"I can't recall ever making this statement about a book: church leaders need this. Nine out of ten churches in North America are in need of some level of significant revitalization. Andy Davis has led true revitalization at one church for two decades. *Revitalize* will guide church leaders for many years to come. Incredible. Inspiring. Biblical."

—**Thom S. Rainer**, president and CEO, LifeWay Christian Resources

"I have served two churches during my lifetime. One was a church revitalization project, the other was a church plant. I can tell you that revitalization takes every bit as much skill, courage, and prayer as church planting. Andy Davis has spent years in revitalization work, and in this book he makes what he has learned accessible to others. I welcome this solid new contribution to the growing literature on helping churches 'come alive again.'"

—**Tim Keller**, founding pastor, Redeemer Presbyterian Church, New York City

"Thousands of churches in the United States are in numerical and spiritual decline. This means the task of church reform and revitalization is one of the church's most urgent needs. For almost two decades, Andy Davis has modeled courage and biblical fidelity in pastoral ministry. He is a pastor who truly knows what it means to see God revitalize a church through the power of his Word. This resource is the culmination of Davis's expansive and biblical wisdom on revitalization. Pastors, no matter how experienced or inexperienced, need to read this book."

—**R. Albert Mohler, Jr.**, president, Southern Baptist Theological Seminary

"Some books contain a fair bit of biblical exposition but tease out rather poorly the implications for church life. Other are larded with practical tips sustained by only the most tenuous links to Scripture. *Revitalize* avoids both of these sad extremes. Born in the furnace of tough experience, this book is simultaneously encouragement and contrition, biblical exhortation and the voice of hard-earned experience, clarity on the gospel and clarity on the church. If you are a pastor and don't need this book at the moment, buy it anyway—the time will come when you will need it."

—**D. A. Carson**, research professor of New Testament, Trinity Evangelical Divinity School

"This is a really good book in so many ways. Pastor Andy Davis is humble and honest, biblical and practical, as he helps us understand what is required to turn around a dying church. And he is an excellent writer, which makes reading *Revitalize* a joy. I will refer to this book again and again in the future because it is a fount of wisdom. I cannot commend it highly enough."

—**Daniel L. Akin**, presi˭˭˭ l Seminary

"*Revitalize* is not for the faint of heart. It will put iron in your backbone at the same time that it calls you to bend your knees before the Lord who alone can build his church. Written by a man of courage and faith, *Revitalize* reflects the realities of pastoral scars while extoling the beauty and power of Christ's wounds to inspire a new generation of pastoral warriors. Don't look for simplistic techniques in these pages, but drink deeply of the pool of Andy Davis's pastoral experience that sparkles with biblical priorities on which Christ builds and rebuilds his church."

—**Bryan Chapell**, pastor, Grace Presbyterian Church

"The American landscape is filled with churches that are plateaued and declining. Thousands of congregations are in need of the sort of spiritual revitalization that can only be led by godly pastors and empowered by the work of the Holy Spirit. For this reason, I'm thrilled that Andy Davis has written this timely book. Andy was my pastor for a decade at First Baptist Church of Durham. The final four of those years we served together as elders, where I witnessed 'up close and personal' the prayerful implementation of the principles found in this book. *Revitalize* offers a great balance of Scriptural principles, real-life stories from the pastoral 'front line,' and practical application. I pray this book becomes a valuable resource and a source of encouragement for pastors and lay leaders who long to see their own churches revitalized."

—**Nathan A. Finn**, dean of the School of Theology and Missions, Union University

"Andy Davis is an amazing man with an amazing story. I watched the revitalization of First Baptist Church of Durham from afar. As I read this book, I was freshly moved by this compelling account of what God did in that place through the faithful labors of this pastor. This book tells that story. *Revitalize* contains not only the story but also many wise and essential lessons about the important work of church revitalization from a thoughtful, courageous pastor who grew from this remarkable journey. I can confidently commend this work, as well as the man who lived it."

—**Brian Croft**, senior pastor, Auburndale Baptist Church; founder, Practical Shepherding; senior fellow, Mathena Center for Church Revitalization, Southern Baptist Theological Seminary

"With a title like *Revitalize: Biblical Keys to Helping Your Church Come Alive Again*, you'd expect a 'manual' of best practices on 'how to' revitalize a plateaued or dying church. Instead, Andy Davis leads us through the Bible, preparing pastors, church leaders, and church members to be the kinds of vessels useful to God in his revitalization project. If you want a best practices book on what *you* can do to revitalize a church, you'll need to look elsewhere. But if you want to be the kind of person *God* uses to revitalize his church, then you've got the right book."

—**Juan R. Sanchez**, senior pastor, High Pointe Baptist Church

REVITALIZE

BIBLICAL KEYS TO HELPING
YOUR CHURCH COME ALIVE AGAIN

ANDREW M. DAVIS

BakerBooks

a division of Baker Publishing Group
Grand Rapids, Michigan

Published by Baker Books
a division of Baker Publishing Group
P.O. Box 6287, Grand Rapids, MI 49516-6287
www.bakerbooks.com

Printed in the United States of America

Library of Congress Cataloging-in-Publication Data
Names: Davis, Andrew M. (Andrew Martin), 1962– author.
Title: Revitalize : biblical keys to helping your church come alive again / Andrew M. Davis.
Description: Grand Rapids : Baker Books, 2017. | Includes bibliographical references.
Identifiers: LCCN 2016041993 | ISBN 9780801007507 (pbk.)
Subjects: LCSH: Church renewal.
Classification: LCC BV600.3 .D38 2017 | DDC 262.001/7—dc23
LC record available at https://lccn.loc.gov/2016041993

Unless otherwise indicated, Scripture quotations are from The Holy Bible, English Standard Version® (ESV®), copyright © 2001 by Crossway, a publishing ministry of Good News Publishers. Used by permission. All rights reserved. ESV Text Edition: 2011

Scripture quotations labeled KJV are from the King James Version of the Bible.

Scripture quotations labeled NASB are from the New American Standard Bible®, copyright © 1960, 1962, 1963, 1968, 1971, 1972, 1973, 1975, 1977, 1995 by The Lockman Foundation. Used by permission. (www.Lockman.org)

17 18 19 20 21 22 23   8 7 6 5 4 3 2

To the faithful pastors who preceded me
and the godly brothers and sisters who prayed for FBC
to be revitalized long before I got here.

Contents

Acknowledgments 9

Foreword by Mark Dever 10

1. Eyes of Blazing Fire: *The Zeal of Christ to Revitalize His Church* 13
2. God Speaks Life into Dying Churches 29
3. Embrace Christ's Ownership of the Church 47
4. Be Holy 58
5. Rely on God, Not on Yourself 71
6. Rely on God's Word, Not on Techniques 78
7. Saturate the Church in Prayer 93
8. Cast a Clear Vision 104
9. Be Humble toward Opponents 114
10. Be Courageous 128
11. Be Patient 138

Contents

12. Be Discerning   154

13. Wage War against Discouragement   162

14. Develop and Establish Men as Leaders   175

15. Become Supple on Worship   186

16. Embrace the Two Journeys of Disciple-Making   198

17. A Heavenly Celebration of God's Glory   212

   Notes   215

Acknowledgments

I am grateful to Mark Dever for the sound guidance on healthy church life at the beginning of my ministry here at First Baptist Church of Durham. I am also thankful for the support of my wife, Christi, and the input from my co-laborer at FBC for seventeen years, Andy Winn, and from my fellow elders at FBC. I also want to acknowledge the help given by Anne Harford and Tom Knight in working to shape the final version of this book. I am grateful to God for all of you!

Foreword

like this book. I like this book for a number of reasons. I like this book because it exalts God. Andy Davis is both ambitious and cautious—ambitious for what God might do and cautious of any talk of what we can do in our own strength. He is convinced that revitalizing a local church is not something he could do himself. He knows that such work is something that only God can do. And this book is clear on that.

I like this book because it is biblically and theologically sound and historically informed. And it's more than that. It is instructive. How many times does a pastor reach for a practical book and find the author is actually carefully and accurately instructing from the Bible? What a wonderful and, sadly, unusual find!

I like this book because the author understands both what the gospel is and what a church is. Those particular matters of theology that come to focus in the local church are clear in this book, and they are combined with lessons from the author's own life. Which brings me to another reason I like this book.

I like this book because it is practical. Some books wrap a single idea or two in 150 or 200 pages. This book is the opposite. Each chapter is stuffed full of ideas that local pastors will understand and can actually use. You don't need to attend special "Andy Davis seminars" to know how to apply the wisdom in this book. Davis's humility and humor help the reader relate to the lessons he has learned and shares.

I like this book because I think it will help pastors. It joins a fairly elite group of books—like C. H. Spurgeon's *Lectures to My Students* and D. Martyn Lloyd-Jones's *Preaching and Preachers*—that combine theology and practice as only a learned and experienced pastor can. Reading this book may well be one of the chief means God uses to not only prevent you from being fired or quitting but also bring new life to your local church. I'm pretty sure Satan won't want you to read this book!

Finally, I like this book because I like Andy Davis. I've known Andy for more than thirty years and have never failed to appreciate his love for God and his confidence in God's Word. I know the story he recounts here to be true. I got the phone calls and letters and had numerous personal visits through the years he describes. And all that he shares here is what I saw and knew in those years. It is a story of real dependence on God and humility so profound it allowed Andy to speak God's Word in confidence even while his flesh was trembling. He shares soberly the challenges but never crosses over into being melodramatic or self-important.

So read this book. Use it as a diagnostic tool in regard to your own church and ministry. It is a Christ-exalting and pastor-encouraging read. Andy Davis's experience is marshalled to serve pastors. This is an important work on an important topic. It is a guidebook that may hold the secret to your own survival. Humility, wisdom, and love are all found in these pages, and you'll need all three to understand and apply the lessons in this book. God may use this book to answer your church's prayers for new life. I pray that is the case. Read and prosper, brother pastor. Read and prosper. And thanks, Andy, for living the life you describe here and for taking the time and effort to share it now with us.

Mark Dever
Pastor, Capitol Hill Baptist Church, Washington DC
Reformation Day (October 31, 2015)

1

Eyes of Blazing Fire

The Zeal of Christ to Revitalize His Church

In the first chapter of Revelation, the apostle John has an awesome vision of the resurrected Christ walking among seven golden lampstands with eyes like blazing fire and his feet like burnished bronze. Christ is dressed in a priestly robe reaching down to his feet, with a golden sash around his chest. Perhaps most striking of all, Christ has a sharp double-edged sword coming from his mouth, and his voice is like the sound of rushing waters. In his right hand he holds seven stars. The seven golden lampstands represent the seven churches in Asia Minor: Ephesus, Smyrna, Pergamum, Thyatira, Sardis, Philadelphia, and Laodicea. The seven stars in his right hand represent the "angels" of these seven churches.

In Revelation 2–3, Christ speaks to each of these seven churches through their respective angels. His messages are powerful, personal, and specific, addressing the strengths and weaknesses of each local church and giving both warnings and encouragements about the future. These seven churches were real local churches that existed during John's time in Asia Minor, near the island of Patmos, where John was in exile. However, there is also a clear sense that they represent Christ's intimate knowledge of and concern for each local church around the world throughout every era of church history. That the churches are depicted as golden lampstands shows their immense worth coupled with their role as lights shining in a dark place. Christ's walking in the midst of these seven golden lampstands illustrates his active concern for the churches, as well as his vigilant and dynamic ministry among them. The seven angels in Christ's right hand illustrate his sovereign power over the pastors of these churches.[1]

How awesome, then, to see the resurrected Christ moving actively through these seven lampstands—tending them, dealing with their pastors, speaking words of comfort or rebuke to them. I submit that this vision, as well as the subsequent letters to the seven churches, represents Christ's ongoing work of church reformation. To some, Christ speaks words of commendation for their tireless labor, doctrinal accuracy, faithfulness in persecution, discernment of error, and hatred of compromise. To others, Christ speaks words of rebuke for their forsaking of their first love, doctrinal compromise, toleration of sinning members, worldliness, spiritual deadness, self-confidence in wealth, and lukewarmness. To all, Christ gives words of exhortation to continue in courageous progress in the gospel, to look to the sweet eternal rewards, and to hear the words God speaks to the churches by the Spirit.

Careful study of the letters to the seven churches provides powerful insight into Christ's zeal for the ongoing revitalization of the church in every age. Revelation 1–3 clearly indicates that the slide of local churches from health toward death has been an ongoing issue for twenty centuries. The church at Ephesus had forsaken its first love, and the Lord threatened to remove its lampstand if they refused to repent (Rev. 2:4–5). The removal of the lampstand is Christ's judgment on any church that, through sin, slides from life to death; Christ sovereignly removes them from the community, and they are gone. He has done this consistently throughout church history. Indeed, history indicates that by the third century, the church at Ephesus had possibly been removed. In any case, it was certainly gone by the time Islam had come to dominate that region of the world in the seventh century. False teachers infiltrated the church at Pergamum, and Christ threatened to come and wage war against them with the sword of his mouth (Rev. 2:14–16). The church at Thyatira was guilty of tolerating sexual immorality, and Christ threatened to throw any who sinned in this way on a sickbed resulting in death (Rev. 2:20–23). The church at Sardis was clearly in need of revitalization. Christ said, "You have the reputation of being alive, but you are dead." And he warned them, "Wake up, and strengthen what remains and is about to die" (Rev. 3:1–2). Perhaps no church of the seven so clearly fits into the pattern of revitalization as that one. The church at Laodicea was lukewarm, and Christ threatened to spew them out of his mouth (Rev. 3:15–16). Local churches have stood in need of revitalization from the beginning of church history.

Truly in the matter of church reformation, the Father is always at his work, even to this very day, while Christ too is working.

Revitalization in Our Generation

The timeless message of Revelation 1–3 must be applied to churches in our generation. Every local church must listen carefully to what the Spirit says to *each* of these seven churches (Rev. 2:7, 11, 17, 29; 3:6, 13, 22). Christ is still walking among the seven golden lampstands with eyes of fire and a sword coming out of his mouth. His zeal for the holiness and fruitfulness of every local church is undiminished. This book is intended to be an instrument in his holy hands for the revitalization of churches all across America, and perhaps even around the world. My desire is to be an encouragement to brothers and sisters, and especially to elders (pastors), who are called to churches needing revitalization. I want to give them some of the insights and convictions the Lord has laid on my heart as I have traveled a journey of revitalization at First Baptist Church (FBC) in Durham, North Carolina. I yearn to root these insights and convictions in passages of Scripture. I also desire to illustrate them with real-life circumstances, both successes and failures, from my own experience. A clear connection between eternal Scripture and temporal circumstances can be a potent prescription for Christians who may be tempted to grow weary in their own journeys of revitalization.

The most powerful weapon in the hands of our Almighty Lord for the destruction of Satan's dark kingdom is a healthy local church. No one knows this better than Satan, and therefore it is expected that he will be vigorously active in fighting reform efforts made in specific local churches. The battle lines are drawn, the enemy is active, and the war is on! As I will discuss later, one of Satan's most powerful weapons is discouragement. He wants to deceive us into thinking that the slow descent of a local church into coldness, doctrinal error, lifeless fellowship, and nonexistent witness in the world is inevitable. He has planted his double agents in dying churches, and these wolves in sheep's clothing are some of the bitterest and most subtle enemies of the gospel. We must expect a fight and not grow weary as it becomes shockingly ugly. Christ is greater, and his Word is sufficient. The goal of a healthy, fruitful Great Commission church is well worth the suffering. This book is written from a deep yearning to equip you for that fight, strengthen your hearts with solid food from God's Word, and guide you with wisdom and clear strategies for victory.

The church scene of the West in the twenty-first century is not encouraging. Christianity is in a decaying orbit in its formerly positive relationship with surrounding culture. Christian views on salvation, the exclusivity of Christ, sexual morality, the sanctity of human life, the nature and permanence of marriage, and the like, are less and less accepted. The steep decline in the health and fruitfulness of many local churches is both a cause and an effect of this decaying orbit. Church health cannot be reduced to baptism, attendance, and budget statistics; however, such numbers can be important indicators of health or disease. The Barna Group has shown that, while the US adult population has grown 15 percent over the last fifteen years, the number of unchurched adults has grown by 92 percent.[2] Mainline denominations (e.g., the United Methodist Church, the Evangelical Lutheran Church in America, the Presbyterian Church (USA), the Episcopal Church, the American Baptist Churches, the United Church of Christ, the Disciples of Christ, et al.) have been seriously in decline in these areas for decades—an aggregate picture of the death of many previously flourishing local churches. Even denominations that have many healthy local churches (like the one our church is affiliated with, the Southern Baptist Convention or SBC) still show a general decline in these areas, and many historically influential churches are in serious need of revitalization. Thom Rainer asserts that somewhere between eight thousand and ten thousand churches close every year.[3] The only remedies to this trend are church planting and church revitalization.

Revitalization vs. Normal Pastoral Ministry

What is "revitalization"? How is it different from normal pastoral ministry in a healthy church? These are key questions. It is not true that every church needs revitalization, for if that were so, the word would lose its distinctive meaning and cease to be helpful. No church is perfect, and every church could grow in faithfulness to Christ. When later I list elements of a healthy church, every true believer in Christ will acknowledge that they long for growth in each of those elements in their local church. Conversely, when I list elements of a church that needs revitalization, it is possible that many healthy churches see some of these reflected in their church life. But there is a composite level of church decline discernible from the elements enumerated below that indicates when a church is in need of revitalization.

One of the easiest ways to measure church vitality is by counting heads—membership and baptisms/conversions. If those numbers are flat (plateaued) or declining each year, that church may well be unhealthy, sliding toward eventual death. Ed Stetzer of LifeWay Research based his book on revitalization, *Comeback Churches*, on studies of three hundred churches that (1) had plateaued and/or declined for five years (worship attendance grew less than 10 percent in a five-year period); and (2) had followed that plateau/decline with significant numerical growth over two to five years, including a membership to baptism (conversion) ratio of 35:1 or lower each year and at least a 10 percent increase in attendance each year.[4] Stetzer grounds the rest of his book on lessons learned by those three hundred churches. Much of the focus for the entire study centers around evangelistic fruit—what he calls being "missional."

However, numerical growth alone cannot be a measure of spiritual health. Some of the unhealthiest churches in the nation are characterized by the false doctrine of the prosperity gospel, but they are huge and growing numerically.[5] Conversely, some churches may be quite healthy in many respects and seeing steady fruit in evangelism but are actually shrinking in number because the godly leadership is culling bloated rolls of past members who, by their chronic failure to attend worship, are displaying in their lives that they most likely were not born again. Other churches might have a good number of people attending and might see some baptisms, but they are toxic in their daily life because of long-standing church politics and unhealthy attitudes and practices. Thus, applying the term *revitalization* requires wisdom and an array of factors must be taken into consideration.

In this book, we will use the word *revitalization* to describe the effort to restore by biblical means a once healthy church from a present level of disease to a state of spiritual health, as defined by the Word of God. I will establish an array of characteristics that define both a healthy church and an unhealthy church, by which church leaders can evaluate their local church. Churches in need of revitalization differ from healthy churches that simply need maturing in that toxic forces are at work that will make ministry there a particular challenge, and if left unchecked, will finally result in the death of the church.

FBC: A Church in Need of Revitalization

One unforgettable Sunday morning at FBC—August 19, 2001—I began corporate worship by calling on the members of the church to repent. The church had elected a female deacon for the first time in its history, which would not be nearly as significant were it not for the fact that our polity at that time saw deacons as lay leaders with shepherding responsibility for the flock alongside the ministerial staff. Despite my church-wide teaching on the topic of gender and authority, and my efforts at the personal level to forestall this result, the church voted in a woman as a spiritual leader.

So I began worship by calling on all the people of FBC to repent—including myself. In the spirit of Daniel 9:7, I felt that all of us must take responsibility for FBC violating God's clear guidance that men should lead in a local church. My call for repentance was an object of horror to many of the members of the church—they were outraged. In their minds, repentance is something you do only at the beginning of the Christian life and then never need to do again (a perversion of the "decisionism"/walk the aisle technique coupled with "once saved, always saved" doctrine). For them, it was as if I were saying, "Because you voted for a woman as a deacon, you are not Christians." But I did not believe that at all. Rather, I know that because of the power of indwelling sin described so clearly in Romans 7, a healthy Christian life is one of constant conviction over sin and repentance from that sin. For me, repentance is a daily, sometimes hourly necessity.

The journey that followed over the next ten years is the context in which the Lord taught me many lessons on church revitalization. FBC had entrenched power structures and un-biblical attitudes in many vital areas, including an unbiblical church government based on committees and democratic processes that resulted in unbiblical lay leadership for de-cades; a large number of influential members whose status as regenerate believers in Christ was at best suspect; a chronic pattern of running off godly pastors who had sought to min-ister well to the church; an unbiblical attitude toward money, with an unhealthy focus on the beauty of the building to the exclusion of missionary efforts; a poor discipleship program; a bad history of racism in dealing with the surrounding com-munity; a clique of powerful lay leaders who considered it their responsibility to dominate church life in secular ways; and a large contingent of senior adults who had received little solid biblical training.

Despite all of that, FBC also had a remnant of extremely godly men and women who were praying and yearning for the revitalization of their beloved church. Without them, I never would have survived the stormy years of war that would soon follow that call for repentance. This is as much their story as it is mine.

A church that stops reforming is dying. And a church that has been in that state for a long time will be rescued only by revitalization. As dangerous and painful as church revitalization can be, the far greater danger is *not* revitalizing. And FBC was a church very much in need of revitalization. In this book, I will seek to relate some of the lessons learned from FBC's journey from the toxic church I began pastoring in 1998 to the encouragingly healthy and fruitful church it is today. The lessons apply to pastors and church members who may be influential in moving their church toward spiritual vitality.

Fourteen Lessons in Revitalization

The lessons that follow will each be the focus of an entire chapter, supported with Scripture and experiential anecdotes. Here they are in summary:

Embrace Christ's ownership of the church. Christ is the only One who shed his blood for the church (Acts 20:28); it is his, for he bought it at a price. A common characteristic of dying churches is an unhealthy sense of ownership of the church by its members and/or leaders. Some feel that because of their financial contributions or hours of service, *This church is mine.* Hence the power struggles. Beyond this, a revitalizing pastor can get sucked into similarly unhealthy thought patterns as he suffers and makes sacrifices for the church. We must embrace, by faith, that the local church is Christ's, and do all our ministry for his glory.

Be holy. Christ's eyes are blazing fire, and his garments are radiant with pure light, representing his perfect holiness. Likewise, the sword coming from his mouth represents his Word in its power to cut the tumor of sin from his church. Everyone committed to revitalization must seek total purity from sin in his life. He must submit his public and private life to the holy gaze of Christ and be humbled and convicted of sin, or he will be disqualified from leading the church toward vitality. Beyond this, he must lead the church to embrace sanctification—consistent growth in holiness by the power of the Spirit.

Rely on God, not on yourself. One of the greatest battles we face in life is learning to rely on God and not on ourselves. If we look toward the perilous journey ahead of us in church reform and then turn inwardly for the resources, we will think either we have what it takes or we do not. The first will result in arrogance; the second will result in despair. Arrogance and despair are two sides of the same coin: self-reliance. We must learn at every moment to look upward to God by faith and rely on his power to do the transformation.

Rely on God's Word, not on techniques. Church revitalization cannot be bought from a Christian bookstore. God's Word must be unleashed, not only weekly from the pulpit but also throughout every ministry and moment of church life. God's Word alone has the power to save souls and bring them to Christlike maturity.

Saturate the church in prayer. Prayer is essential to the revitalization of a dying church. Through prayer, we fully rely on God and acknowledge our powerlessness to effect the many changes that will need to be made. Prayer changes us and also mysteriously changes things by the sovereign power of God. Pastors must personally become men of prayer more than ever before, and they must also call the godly together for fervent prayer, otherwise the church will not be revitalized.

Cast a clear vision. Leaders must make clear to the congregation what God wants the church to be—both in the big picture and in the details. This vision must come from Scripture and from the specific calling God places on that congregation. Leaders must powerfully cast this vision week after week to the church and lead the church toward it by the power of the Spirit and the ministry of the Word. Leaders must especially be effective in helping other key leaders see this biblical vision for the church.

Be humble toward opponents. "God opposes the proud, but gives grace to the humble" (James 4:6). In the struggle to revitalize a local church, it is easy to demonize opponents and slander them privately. It is easy to play political battles and lower your ethical standards, all the while forgetting that you are every bit as sinful as they are apart from the sovereign grace of God in Christ. God commands that we be humble and loving toward all who oppose us and allow his Word to transform them as it is transforming us.

Be courageous. Satan will fight the revitalization every step of the way and will use people to attack any who are working for the transformation of the church. Fear of man is one of the biggest snares that Satan casts on our path. Learning how to conquer our fear and live only to please God is vital, for the road ahead takes courage. Courage comes from the Word of God and the power of the Spirit. God also uses the examples of suffering heroes from church history to give us the ability to stand strong in our day of testing. While the previous lesson says we must resist the temptation to be arrogant toward opponents, this lesson says we must resist the opposite temptation to be cowardly. When the time comes to act boldly, we must act!

Be patient. The work of church revitalization is slow, requiring a great deal of patience. It is fascinating how many of Jesus's parables are agricultural, likening the work of the kingdom of God to plants growing from the earth. In James 5, the farmer has learned to be patient, waiting for God to give the growth. In the same way, we must give God time to work in people's hearts by the steady progress of his Word.

Be discerning. The previous two points—be courageous and be patient—seem to be contradictory. When do we move out boldly and when do we wait on the Lord? Discernment is needed. Additionally, churches have notoriously squabbled over an array of minor points. It is essential that godly leaders be discerning regarding what issues are worth drawing a line in the sand.

Wage war against discouragement. One of Satan's primary weapons against a work of revitalization is discouragement. He is constantly whispering in the ear of key leaders in the church that the changes desired will never come to fruition. We must constantly be of good courage and know that our final victory is guaranteed and that our labor in the Lord is not in vain (1 Cor. 15:58). A godly leader must be so filled with hope and confidence in God that he can inspire the same in others.

Develop and establish men as leaders. This practical and biblical step was a strategic key to the revitalization of FBC Durham. It is also vital to God's overall strategy for the church in the world. God has entrusted the leadership of the church to men, and those men need to be identified, equipped, and empowered to lead. A single pastor, fighting on his own against the entrenched forces that have caused the church's decline, will almost certainly lose. As God raises up men to join him, the burdens of leadership and suffering become greatly lessened through sharing. Since God has ordained a plurality of elders to lead churches, even if that polity is not yet established, an early and provisional version of it during the revitalization phase is immeasurably helpful and a major step in the right direction.

Become supple on worship. Christ used a dual analogy of wineskins and patches of cloth (Matt. 9:16–17) to teach a clear lesson about the dynamic kingdom of God: stay supple, yield, stretch as God is making changes. Churches in need of revitalization are usually stuck in the past, in traditionalism, in "the way we've always done it around here." This is especially true in worship style. But the church that refuses to stay connected with surrounding culture musically will usually cease to be appealing to younger believers and will tend to age upward. Church leaders need to make clear distinctions between what is timeless in church life (e.g., the gospel, biblical doctrines, etc.) and what is temporary (e.g., choirs, pipe organs, specific hymns sung a specific way, etc.).

Embrace the two journeys of disciple-making. Christ has left us on Earth to glorify God by making disciples. Disciple-making comes in two discernable ways: the internal journey of growth into Christlike maturity and the external journey of worldwide evangelism and missions. These two journeys must be held in balance. A church that never sees lost people converted, baptized, and taught to obey Christ's commandments is a church that has died. Conversely, when revitalization starts taking hold, more and more members of the church will display a sacrificial heart for the lost in their prayers, conversations, and lives. This is a crowning element of all true works of revitalization. A pastor who yearns to see revitalization in a local church must make a steady appeal to God to work in him and the church a passion for the lost.

May God Strengthen You for This Work

Some who read this book will be in dwindling rural churches with senior adults who are hardly contentious but also hardly motivated to do much beyond the status quo. Some will be in larger urban churches that have virulent factions ready for war. Some will be in churches that have been in numerical decline for years, with no clear indication as to why. Some will be in suburban settings with relatively new facilities that are unpaid for and debt that is strangling the church. Some will be in churches whose previous pastors have all but killed the church with immorality or wretchedly bad leadership. Some will be in churches in communities that are economically depressed and have seen a great migration to other locales with better employment opportunities. Some will be in "family chapel" churches dominated by the political and financial power of a single family or a small cluster of families who desire control rather than numerical growth. The variety of case studies of church revitalizations over the last thirty years could be enumerated at length. No one book can speak to the specific strategies and detailed sequences of actions that will inexorably lead to church revitalization in all of these individual cases.

However, it is my prayer that God will use this book to give you hope that he can do amazing work before your eyes. The revitalization of your church could end up being the most significant act of service you will ever render to Christ. The resurrected and glorified Christ is still moving through the golden lampstands of his churches, speaking words of counsel and rebuke, wisdom and encouragement to each one of his blood-bought churches. Though in his sovereign power he has the right to remove any of these lampstands, it may well be that he has raised you up for such a time as this—to be an instrument in his hand for the revitalization of a dying church to become a light shining radiantly in an incredibly dark world.

2

God Speaks Life into Dying Churches

I have been in the handsome carcasses of dead churches in many places throughout the world. Recently, I took a tour of the astonishingly beautiful cathedral of St. Vitus in Prague, Czech Republic. The construction of this particular building began in 1344 and continued over the next five centuries. It is a breathtaking display of Gothic architecture, with some truly stunning stained glass portrayals of scenes from the Bible and church history. But it stands in one of the most godless nations on Earth,[1] and according to our tour guide, no vibrant congregation meets there now. It is more or less a museum of human artistic achievement. It was not much different in the church I toured in Eisleben, Germany, where Martin Luther preached his last sermon, or the impressive cathedral I saw in Amsterdam that is now a boutique for avant-garde clothing fashions or the little white former church in South Hamilton, Massachusetts, which had become an art store. In the same way, a friend of mine, Jan Vezikov, is planting a church in Boston and is pressed to find a space for his growing and vibrant new congregation. He drives by dozens of church buildings in the city that are effectively vacant on Sunday mornings but whose trustees won't sell or allow the building to be used for worship by another congregation.

As I mentioned in the opening chapter, it is clear that many congregations across our country are dying (or are already dead). They stand on valuable real estate and are housed in structures that have commercial value. If any people still attend them on Sunday mornings, they may well be some of the hardest people to reach with the genuine gospel of Jesus Christ. Many eager young laborers for the Lord question that they should spill the blood of their souls in revitalizing such a congregation. It seems much more efficient to plant a new church in a new location. So many questions about revitalization exist right from the start. This chapter will seek to answer those preliminary questions and lay the groundwork for all that follows.

What Is Revitalization?

The word *revitalize* could be expanded into a phrase—to make alive again. Revitalization occurs when God restores a once healthy church, helping it to change course from its recent decline toward spiritual disease and death. The title of this book is in the imperative form: *Revitalize*. Because God alone gives life, he must give the command or it will never happen. *Revitalize* is a word that God speaks to the dry bones of a dead church or to the weak, helpless form of a dying church. Both images come from the book of Ezekiel. In the case of a dead church, it is just as God did to the dry bones of the nation of Israel in Ezekiel 37: "Thus says the Lord GOD to these bones: Behold, I will cause breath to enter you, and you shall live" (v. 5), and "Thus says the Lord GOD: Come from the four winds, O breath, and breathe on these slain, that they may live" (v. 9). Similarly, in Ezekiel 16 God said he found Jerusalem as an infant lying by the side of the road, helpless and dying, and brought her to life with his Word: "And when I passed by you and saw you wallowing in your blood, I said to you in your blood, 'Live!' I said to you in your blood, 'Live!'" (v. 6). So every revitalization of a church from dying or dead is an act of the sovereign God of the universe who speaks the powerful, life-giving word to the church: "Live!" or "Be revitalized!" And since God alone can do this, the first human action in this work must be a prayer to God to work this miracle: "Revitalize, O Lord!"

Also, though, God raises up leaders whom he uses to do this work. He gives them a vision for the transformation of their local church and also the role they must play. He calls pastors to begin preaching life-giving messages that are used in the spiritual transformation of the people. Note in Ezekiel 37 that God raised up the prophet Ezekiel to speak God's words to the dry bones, to command them in the name of the Lord, "Live!" So also God uses godly leaders to speak his words powerfully to a dying or dead church to make it come alive again. The imperative form, "Revitalize!" comes echoing back from God to those who pray it. God commands us to rise up and "Revitalize!"—to act powerfully by the Holy Spirit to effect this amazing change.

Revival and Revitalization

What is the relationship between revitalization and revival? Many evangelical churches talk about revival a great deal. They pray for it, yearn for it, and preach so that it will come about. And ever since the day of Pentecost, the church has sought an outpouring of the Holy Spirit resulting in greater holiness and evangelistic power. Many scholars have sought to put into words exactly what a revival is:

- "God's quickening visitation of his people, touching their hearts and deepening his work of grace in their lives." —J. I. Packer[2]

- "The sovereign act of God, in which He restores His own backsliding people to repentance, faith and obedience." —Stephen Olford[3]

- "The work of the Holy Spirit in restoring the people of God to a more vital spiritual life, witness, and work by prayer and the Word after repentance in crisis for their spiritual decline." —Earle Cairns[4]

As one looks over these definitions, it's interesting to note that none of them speak directly of the massive evangelistic fruit that one usually associates with revival. Charles Spurgeon explains why:

We could not speak of the *re*-vival of a thing which never lived before. It is clear that the term "revival" can only be applied to a living soul, or to that which once lived. To be revived is a blessing which can only be enjoyed by those who have some degree of life. Those who have no spiritual life are not, and cannot be, in the strictest sense of the term, the subjects of a revival. Many blessings may come to the unconverted in consequence of a revival among Christians, but the revival itself has to do only with those who already possess spiritual life. There must be vitality in some degree before there can be a quickening of vitality, or, in other words, a revival. A true revival is to be looked for in the church of God.[5]

So in the end, one could argue that *revival* and *revitalization* are really words for the same thing. Perhaps the only difference might be the spiritual heights to which the revitalized church soars in fervor and in evangelistic fruit. But that is a matter of degree, not of essential nature.

Why Revitalize?

In every generation, God raises up Spirit-filled, visionary, passionate, and capable young men and calls them into full-time work as pastors (elders). As they are completing their training, the time draws near for them to be decisive about what kind of work God is calling them to do. Is it cross-cultural missions? Or is it here in North America? If the former, are they called to plant a new church or to work in an existing church? If the latter, are they called into an essentially healthy church or to work in a dysfunctional, unhealthy, dying church? The more one considers the options, the more it becomes obvious that a clear defense for church revitalization would be helpful. What could possibly motivate a person to embrace the kind of suffering and exasperating trials that inevitably come with revitalization?

The advantages of church planting seem obvious: the freedom to establish the church from the beginning, according to the "recipe" the church planters have embraced; the freedom to write the constitution and bylaws and set up the worship service and preaching style accordingly; the knowledge that all the people who commit to that church after sampling its ministry are doing so in glad-hearted support of the recipe of ministry the new church has established; the unity and joy of reaching the unchurched in that community with the gospel, of seeing the lost coming to faith in Christ, etc. Along with that is the freedom from the power struggles and corrupt history that characterize a dying church, and freedom from the unregenerate church members who have contributed mightily to that church's decay.

So why should a visionary young leader give his best years to a dying church? Here are some reasons:

(1) *To bring glory to God by doing something difficult for the kingdom.* No ministry of eternal consequence is easy, and each display of valor for the glory of God will shine in heaven with its own radiance. Overcoming the specific obstacles that attend the revitalization of a local church brings a unique kind of glory to God.

(2) *To restore Christ's reputation in a community.* Every church assembled under the banner of Christ Jesus affects the reputation of Christ in that community. A dying/dead church is a great dishonor to Christ. As Romans 2:24 puts it, "The name of God is blasphemed among the Gentiles because of you." Ultimately this is why Christ removes lampstands of corrupted churches—their darkness defiles his holy name. But how great is Christ's glory when a church is brought from a deathly decline into a healthy biblical ministry! The onlooking world may be enabled to see the glory of Christ in healing that church.

(3) *To write new chapters to a long story*. It is a glorious thing for God to turn around the unfolding story of a congregation and write an excellent continuation rather than a dishonorable ending. Every local church has its heritage, with its specific heroes and glorious moments. How tragic if that story takes a turn for the worse permanently, never to recover. But how marvelous when God adds some chapters that no one could have foreseen—a satisfying continuation to all that he's done for decades (if not for centuries) in that local church.

(4) *To win the lost in that church*. Every dying church has in it human beings, created in the image of God. The unregenerate members of that church are categorically among the hardest to reach on Earth, because they have heard the Word of God repeatedly without yet having repented. But it is quite possible that God could use a specific servant to bring some unregenerate church members to faith in Christ. And there may be some, perhaps among the senior adults, who have never really heard the gospel clearly and winsomely explained. God may revitalize that church by bringing people like this to a saving faith in Christ, and that alone is worth all the effort and suffering.

(5) *To use that existing platform to win the lost in the community*. That church is already known and established in the community; there is no need to start an ad campaign to announce its existence. Now, as I said in number 2, the church may have a bad reputation in the community, but it is at least a recognizable presence. If God were to revitalize that long-standing member of the civic scene, he could use that existing platform to win the lost in the community.

(6) *To disciple and shepherd the Christians in that church*. The church at Pergamum included some who were still alive

and about to die who needed to wake up and make their deeds complete in God's sight (Rev. 3:2). This represents regenerate but spiritually immature people who populate dying churches, and God may desire to pour out his sanctifying grace on them, bringing them to much higher levels of spiritual maturity than they even dreamed were possible. There also may be some godly and passionate church members who have been like "a voice crying in the wilderness" for many years and who have stayed there waiting for the transformation for which they have been praying fervently. They need godly men who will preach and teach them the Word of God and shepherd their souls. Out of love for them, God may revitalize the church.

(7) *To keep the building, finances, and other ministry materials from being wasted.* Every year, thousands of churches die, and their buildings, finances, and equipment are liquidated and handed over to outsiders. What a waste! It is especially poignant given the fact that church planters know acutely how difficult it is to find a suitable and affordable place to worship. The revitalization of a local church will validate the vision of an earlier generation of godly men and women who sacrificed time, energy, and money to build the building that would be lost if the church were to die. After the feeding of the five thousand, Jesus commanded, "Gather up the leftover fragments, that nothing may be lost" (John 6:12). If Jesus showed such concern for the spiritual value of leftover fragments of barley loaves and fish that no one wanted, surely he would similarly desire that an entire building that once housed a vibrant congregation not be wasted?

(8) *To be a light to other dying churches.* The downward spiral of so many churches ends in final tragedy. Imagine if

no church was ever reclaimed from such a pattern. Imagine if once certain symptoms appear in your local church, there is absolutely no cure—death is certain. But if God shows his power and grace in the renewal of some key churches, would that not give hope to others to strive for the transformation of their church as well?

(9) *To display Christ's love and perseverance in not giving up on his bride.* Christ's tender patience in not giving up on a badly straying church is well worth putting on display. "May the Lord direct your hearts to the love of God and to the steadfastness of Christ" (2 Thess. 3:5).

(10) *To be sanctified in ways specific to this mission.* The work of a church revitalizer is extremely difficult. You will search your soul and cry out in prayer in unprecedented ways. God is not done saving you and the elect in your church. (See 1 Timothy 4:16 for this clear statement: "You will save both yourself and your hearers.") The hard journey ahead will leave you more dependent on Christ and more in awe of his patience, love, and power than ever before.

(11) *To bring about a lovingly multigenerational congregation.* Most of the church plants I know tend to be rather homogenous age-wise, with few senior adults. Rather it is often a team of like-minded, zealous young people. However, the New Testament portrays a church that is multi-generational, with older men and women together with young men, women, and growing children, hence Paul's directions to Titus concerning older men and women in Titus 2:2–3. The power of a multigenerational church is indescribable. The older counterbalance the younger, and vice versa, each having their strengths and weaknesses. Generally speaking, the younger tend to be passionate, energetic, idealistic,

hope-filled—but lacking wisdom and the resources needed to realize their dreams. Conversely, the older tend to be wise, experienced, wealthy, mature—but lacking energy, motivation, and short-term missional vision and hope. "Iron sharpens iron" (Prov. 27:17), so young and old Christians sharpen one another. Revitalizing a dying church often results in a beautiful multigenerational blend.

What Are Marks of a Healthy Church?

In 2004, Mark Dever published his seminal book, *Nine Marks of a Healthy Church*.[6] In this book, he helpfully defines characteristics of healthy churches, establishing measures by which leaders and members alike can evaluate their church for areas of weakness. *Nine Marks*, then available only in pamphlet form, was one of the greatest helps to me in the early stages of my ministry at FBC. The book became a road map of church revitalization for me. Here is my brief restatement of Dever's nine marks in light of church revitalization:

(1) *Expositional preaching.* Healthy pulpits lead to healthy churches, and in a healthy church, the pulpit ministry consistently strives to proclaim and apply the main point of the text as the main point of the sermon. Many churches in need of revitalization have suffered under a chaotic form of topical preaching in which the pastor's whims governed the delivery week after week.

(2) *Biblical theology.* This refers to the consistent and patient teaching of all the truth in the Bible, seeking to give people a sense of the overarching narrative of the Bible and its key doctrinal themes. Central to this is the doctrine of

the inspiration and authority of the Bible—what some call "inerrancy." The Bible is wholly perfect, inspired by God through the Holy Spirit (2 Tim. 3:16). Generally, biblical authority completely unravels if people do not embrace inerrancy. In churches needing revitalization, the congregation's biblical knowledge is shallow and disjointed. They are used to milk, not meat, and often recoil in shocked surprise if someone shows them some of the stronger truths in the Bible.

(3) *Biblical understanding of the gospel.* Healthy churches proclaim the biblical gospel of salvation from God's wrath through repentance and faith in Jesus Christ, asserting his exclusivity as the only Savior for the world (Acts 4:12). Dying churches often have turned to a false gospel.

(4) *Biblical understanding of conversion.* Healthy churches understand what it means to be born again by the Holy Spirit into a new life in Christ and proclaim that this conversion must happen for the sinner to be saved. The more mature a church becomes, the more clearly the marks of regeneration (ways by which people can test themselves to see if they are in the faith; see 2 Cor. 13:5) are preached and understood.

(5) *Biblical understanding of evangelism.* This flows from the previous two marks. A church that rightly understands the gospel and how individuals are saved also seeks to proclaim the message of the gospel plainly in the power of the Holy Spirit to win the lost (Rom. 1:16). Healthy churches avoid gimmicks and worldly techniques to attract a crowd. The healthier the church, the more active they are in sharing the gospel boldly and the more evangelistic fruit they will see. Dying churches almost universally have turned away from bold and fruitful evangelism.

(6) *Biblical understanding of membership.* Embracing a commitment to covenant membership is essential to healthy church life; where members often miss worship services or do not use their gifts to build the church, the church cannot be healthy. Almost every dying church I have ever encountered has a defective view of church membership and a lax approach to its church rolls, which are filled with the names of unregenerate church members—nominal Christians, or what the Puritans called "gospel hypocrites."[7] Most unregenerate church members simply don't attend church; but some are very active in the church and have been instrumental in killing a congregation with their false doctrine and worldly motives.

(7) *Biblical church discipline.* A commitment to faithful church discipline is essential to weeding out unhealthy (unrepentantly sinful) members, thus keeping the entire body protected from the spread of corruption. It is nearly unheard of that a dying church would actually practice biblical church discipline. Implementing biblical patterns of addressing sin in the life of the members is not going to be the first step toward revitalization (any new pastor who tries will soon be evicted!). However, all healthy churches deal with sin in the patterns taught in the New Testament.

(8) *Promotion of church discipleship and growth.* The individual members of healthy churches must grow consistently into spiritual maturity by the ministry of the Word; churches that have no plan or pattern for discipleship cannot be healthy.

(9) *Biblical understanding of leadership.* Many churches have taken their cues on leadership from the world, the very thing Christ told us not to do (Matt. 20:25–26). Rather, healthy

churches are led by a plurality of elders who have been filtered by the biblical criteria of 1 Timothy 3:1–7 and Titus 1:5–9 and whose ministries as servant leaders follow the pattern of Christ.

These nine marks are insightful as a road map for church revitalization. Let me now add a further word on a central theme of FBC's quest for spiritual health.

The Two Infinite Journeys

At the end of this book, I will make the case that every church exists to bring glory to God by making progress in two infinite journeys: the internal journey of sanctification (growth in holiness in conformity to Christ) and the external journey (evangelization and missions). I call them journeys because we must make progress in them (Phil. 1:12, 25). And I call them "infinite" not because we will not complete them, but because they will never be finished while the Lord gives us more time on Earth; only by his infinite power through the Holy Spirit will they be finished. The scriptural evidence for these two journeys is strong. Jesus said, "I am the way, and the truth, and the life. No one comes to the Father except through me" (John 14:6). By using the word *way*, Jesus was asserting that there is a journey one must travel to reach the Father—and Jesus himself is that journey. The internal journey of sanctification is found in Peter's command to "grow in the grace and knowledge of our Lord and Savior Jesus Christ. To him be the glory both now and to the day of eternity!" (2 Pet. 3:18). The external journey is found in many places in the New Testament (Matt. 28:18–20; Mark 16:15–16; John 20:21–23; Acts 1:8). I prefer the depiction of the gospel's journey from Jerusalem to the ends of the earth found in Luke 24:47–48: "Repentance and forgiveness of sins should be preached in his name to all nations, beginning from Jerusalem. You are witnesses of these things."

Healthy churches do *both* of these. They make disciples, *and* they baptize them and teach them to obey all the things that Christ has commanded (Matt. 28:19–20).

What Are Marks of a Church Needing Revitalization?

These marks of a healthy church represent the goal of all church revitalization. However, most patients come to doctors seeking treatment because of some symptoms of disease. Indeed, when I asked two doctors about how they define health, they both said, "It is the absence of disease!" When we say that a church is healthy, we are not saying it is perfect. Just because a church is not perfect does not mean it needs revitalization. There is a threshold of spiritual functionality below which the word *revitalize* is appropriate. What are the marks of a dying or dead church?[8]

(1) *Low view of Scripture.* Churches needing revitalization have in some sense despised the Word of God and turned away from God's messengers in rebellion. They question both the inerrancy and sufficiency of Scripture. This could be displayed by pastors preaching man-centered, topical messages or by the congregation rejecting and driving away godly men who are preaching the Word faithfully. This low view of Scripture shows itself in the biblical ignorance of most of its members and the fact that they can scarcely handle the milk of Scripture, while inevitably choking on the meat.

(2) *Man-centered rather than God-centered.* The church should exist for the glory of God—to put God's perfections radiantly on display. Instead, the dying church lives for its own glory, reputation, agenda, and ideals. It cares much more what key people think than what God thinks, as revealed in his Word.

(3) *Lax shepherding of members and no church discipline.* Dying churches are rife with unregenerate church members. For years, these churches have ignored whether their members are living godly lives. They have had low standards regarding who joins the church. Members' children who give some profession of faith and are baptized at a young age, but who are not walking with Christ in their adulthood, are sentimentally kept on the church rolls. The same happens with people who joined the church years ago, but now no one knows their whereabouts. The more active members are not being shepherded carefully by the pastors, so patterns of sin are not detected early and addressed biblically. And church discipline has not been practiced in years—or perhaps ever.

(4) *Little evangelistic fruit resulting in dwindling numbers.* Jesus came to "seek and to save the lost" (Luke 19:10), but dying churches are not joining Jesus in his mission. Because of their selfishness, worldliness, and sin, dying churches have long since ceased being effective witnesses in their communities. They have little connection to their surrounding neighbors, and if they do, it is in a pattern of worldly "good works" (like United Way), with no connection to the exclusive gospel of Jesus Christ. They are not making disciples, not baptizing them, and not teaching them to obey Christ's commands.

(5) *Disunity and bitter factions.* The dying church is usually bitterly divided, characterized by selfish factions that

feud with one another. Jesus said, "By this all men will know that you are my disciples, if you have love for one another" (John 13:35). It was said of the ancient church that spiritually conquered the Roman Empire, "Behold, how they love one another!"[9] Yet dying churches bite and devour one another (Gal. 5:15). Part of this is the influence of central, ungodly leaders—either men or women—who sow seeds of discord for the sake of their own selfish agendas.

(6) *Disrespect for godly leaders, resulting in short pastorates.* Godly churches love the elders whom God has set in authority over them and hold them in the highest honor because of their work (1 Thess. 5:13; 1 Tim. 5:17). The faction-ridden church almost always fights godly leadership, refusing to submit to its authority (Heb. 13:17). They make life miserable for the pastors unless they tickle their ears with entertaining and soothing sermons (2 Tim. 4:3). Because such a church cannot attract more seasoned godly men, this almost always results in short pastorates occupied by a series of younger pastors who are just beginning their careers in ministry.

(7) *Disorderly polity.* Dying churches ripped apart by factions who do not respect godly authority end up running the church according to their own ideas. The most influential leaders in the church are frequently successful in the world and use worldly leadership techniques to dominate the church. Instead of following the pattern of plural elders and deacons who meet the filtering criteria of 1 Timothy 3:1–13, they establish extrabiblical structures (like a "church council" or a "personnel committee") to suit their own ideas. Often the selfish ambitions of a few people dominate their government. James 3:16 says, "For where jealousy and selfish ambition exist, there will be disorder and every vile practice."

God's Word brings order and unity; worldly ambition brings disorder and sin.

(8) *Clinging to traditions, stubbornly unwilling to change.* Dying churches spend much time pining over the "glory days" of the past. They have "Heritage Days" or cling to traditions whose utility has long since ended. They tend to be prideful about these traditions and fiercely defend them. Their worship style clings to old music patterns that no longer connect with the community or with young people.

(9) *Selfish spending patterns.* Dying churches are essentially selfish, and that is proven by how they spend their money. They spend very little on evangelism, missions, or relief for the poor. Thom Rainer noted one dying church that spent 98 percent of its annual budget on itself.[10] This selfishness extends beyond money to the programs in the church and the energy that church workers expend—they spend on themselves.

(10) *Little zeal for corporate prayer.* Dying churches do not pray together. If the leaders call them to extraordinary prayer meetings, very few come. The things prayed for in public tend to be worldly or connected only with the physical health of dying members. When I came to FBC, we had a Wednesday night meal followed by a prayer meeting. When the time came to pray, many people continued eating and talking with one another. Some who did join the prayer time used to "tsk" and sigh when I would break them into smaller groups to pray for missions. Thank God there was a godly remnant at FBC who did yearn to pray. They were essential to what God did to turn the church around.

(11) *Increasingly worldly doctrines and behaviors.* Because of the initial mark in this list—low view of Scripture—dying

churches hold increasingly worldly views about everything. They especially stagger at controversial teachings in the Bible, namely, God's sovereignty in salvation, the exclusivity of Christ, personal holiness, divorce/remarriage, homosexuality, abortion, et al. Surprisingly, some of these people may be respected senior citizens who are beloved for their civic service in community groups, but they think like the world. The members also live worldly lives characterized by the pursuit of worldly goals like money, possessions, power, and pleasures.

God Speaks Life to Dying Churches

This chapter has unfolded foundational issues that every revitalizing church leader needs to address. I have sought to define revitalization and identify it as revival by the Holy Spirit. I have made a defense for why a painful and costly effort such as revitalization should be undertaken. I also have given a clear description of both healthy and dying churches. But all this information will do nothing to renew a dying church unless the Lord breathes life into it. God alone has the power to do this. It has been my pleasure to watch God speak life into FBC, a church that had many godly people and a series of godly pastors, but which also had the "death rattle" of an increasingly unbiblical direction led by worldly lay leaders and an increasingly potent disrespect for the inerrant Word of God. The conditions in your church may be significantly different, but the same God can speak life into your church as he has into FBC.

3

Embrace Christ's Ownership of the Church

In 1994, I was serving as a missionary in Japan. Early one morning, I stood on a beach and looked out over the ocean to see the blazing sun shed its orange rays across the waves of the Pacific Ocean. I thought about Japan being called the "Land of the Rising Sun," and I prayed that the light of the glory of God in the face of Christ would shine in Japanese hearts (2 Cor. 4:6). I realized that the radiant beauty of those sunbeams had traveled ninety-three million miles through empty space to communicate the immense power of the sun to my eye. Christ is "the radiance of the glory of God and the exact imprint of his nature, and he upholds the universe by the word of his power" (Heb. 1:3). Just as the sunbeams communicate the existence and attributes of the sun to our eyes, so Christ perfectly communicates the being and nature of God to us by faith. That is why, when Philip said to Jesus,

"Show us the Father," Jesus answered, "Have I been with you so long, and you still do not know me, Philip?" (John 14:8–9). Anyone who has seen Jesus has seen the Father. It would be like saying to the sunbeam, "Show us the sun!" The beam would answer, "That is what I came ninety-three million miles across space to do!" And Hebrews 1:3 also tells us that when Christ had atoned for sin, he sat down at the right hand of God in heaven. This radiant, glorious Christ is the head of the church, ruling over all things for the sake of his body (Eph. 1:22–23). As I stood there on that Japanese beach, surrounded by the largest unreached people group on the earth at that time, I yearned for God to exalt Christ on Earth as he is exalted in heaven.

A passion for the exaltation of Christ as head over the church must enflame the heart of all church revitalizers. You must burn with a passion for the supremacy of Christ in your local church. Churches need revitalization precisely because they have become increasingly cold toward the glory of Christ and increasingly dominated by man's glory, wisdom, efforts, agenda, and power. If a church is to be revitalized, then the absolute ownership of the church by Christ must be central to everything you yearn for and do.

Christ Alone Bought This Church with His Blood

One of the most intimidating obstacles I faced in the early years of my ministry at FBC was the assumed authority of those who had been at the church for decades and, thus, considered the church to be their own because they had poured so much money, time, and energy into it. I noticed at church conferences and committee meetings that older people who had been members for more than twenty-five years were apologizing and kowtowing to members who had been at the church for forty years or more. It was as if you were not a full member until you were in the fifty-year club! This attitude of ownership based on squatter's rights was a direct challenge to the supremacy of Christ and to any efforts at church revitalization. These older members had arrogated to themselves an absurd role of authority based on longevity and financial investment, and I felt the need like Boniface to take an axe and chop down this "sacred oak."[1]

Therefore, one Sunday morning, I preached a sermon from Revelation 1 about the supremacy of Christ over all local churches. I spoke of how Christ alone owns every local church, how he alone has the right to walk through the seven golden lampstands and speak words of commands to each church. I expanded to include concepts from other parts of Scripture as well. In Acts 20:28, Paul called on the Ephesian elders to "care for the church of God, which he obtained with his own blood." I directly applied these concepts to FBC. I stated that not one of the members had shed their blood for the church; Christ alone had been with the church every day of its existence since it was founded in 1845. Christ alone had guided the church through every decade, and he alone had gathered all of the departed saints into his eternal presence. FBC was *Christ's*, for he alone had shed his blood for the church. The more I preached on this theme, the bolder and more confident I became. The exaltation of Christ as the sole owner of the church was the power for the revitalization that would follow.

The Bride Belongs to the Bridegroom

Recently I had the pleasure of officiating the wedding of my son Nathaniel to his beautiful bride, Dorothy. At a dramatic moment in the ceremony, the doors at the back of the church swung open and everyone stood up. Dorothy, escorted by her father, made her way to the front of the church with every eye on her. Her dress was spectacular, her hair was perfect, her makeup was flawless, and her jewelry was sparkling. Though everyone was looking at her as she processed forward, my son stared at her with the special anticipation of knowing that she was presenting herself to him to be his bride. Every Christian marriage is a mysterious picture of the perfect union between Christ and his bride, the church (Eph. 5:32). And every Christian wedding is a foretaste of the future union of the perfected church with the bridegroom, Christ.

Nonetheless, there is a significant difference between an earthly wedding and the perfect one that is yet to come. In American culture, the bridegroom contributes nothing to the beautification of the bride on the wedding day. As a matter of fact, tradition dictates that he not even see her until that moment at the wedding ceremony. But Christ, our bridegroom, has been getting his bride ready for the wedding day for centuries, "That he might sanctify her, having cleansed her by the washing of water with the word, so that he might present the church to himself in splendor, without spot or wrinkle or any such thing, that she might be holy and without blemish" (Eph. 5:26–27). Christ's zeal for the perfection of his bride is infinite, as was the cost he paid to make her radiant. Christ will not keep silent or rest (Isa. 62:1–5) until his bride is perfect; he will keep washing her with the Word until she is radiantly glorious, ready for the wedding day. Her glory is his glory, her radiance is his. All her righteous acts are the clean, white linen she wears (Rev. 19:8), and all of them were worked in her by Christ. The New Jerusalem *descends* from heaven, gloriously dressed for the wedding (Rev. 21:2, 10), showing that the adornment of the bride is Christ's work.

Church revitalization is part of Christ's efforts at beautifying his church for his own pleasure, for their wedding day. Thus, a church leader should say, as John the Baptist did, "The one who has the bride is the bridegroom" (John 3:29). The efforts made by a godly pastor at preaching and leading toward revitalization are in service to the bridegroom, to get the bride ready for Christ alone.

The Church Revitalizer Is Nothing; Christ Is Everything

Another great benefit of embracing Christ's ownership of the church is the humility and security it offers to the servants he uses to renew the church. First, the more church leaders delight in the infinite exaltation of Christ and his rights over his vineyard (another metaphor for the church—see Matt. 21:33–43), the more humble they will be about their own roles. As Paul put it, "I planted, Apollos watered, but God gave the growth. So neither he who plants nor he who waters is anything, but only God who gives the growth" (1 Cor. 3:6–7). Church revitalization is like the renewing of a dormant, seemingly dead plant to bear fruit. Not one pastor or lay leader could ever bring this about. This is something only God can do through Christ by the power of the Spirit.

Revitalization is like seeing the life-giving sap flowing from the vine to the branches again, bearing good fruit for Christ. Apart from Jesus, we can do nothing (John 15:5). How, then, can we boast when we are nothing and did nothing? This theme is greatly humbling, and we need great humbling! If the Lord should end up doing the great work of revitalizing your dying church, and if you are tempted to take credit for it, just read 1 Corinthians 3:6–7 again and remember your place. Give him all the glory!

This theme also has the power to protect us from taking criticism too seriously. As the work is progressing, Satan will rouse his servants to bring fierce opposition and poignant criticism, and some of those flaming arrows will find their mark with stinging potency. But as Moses said to the bitter Israelites, "What are we? Your grumbling is not against us but against the Lord!" (Exod. 16:8). We are nothing! If we are standing on Scripture and leading the church toward spiritual health, the opposition is to Christ, not to us. My opponents at FBC did not even know my name two years before that time, and the only reason they were yelling at me in church conferences was because of the Lord's work. I am nothing; Christ is everything.

Marching Orders Come from Christ the King

All servants of the Lord need to be continually reminded that Christ is King, and they are not. We need to bow our knees before his kingship and take marching orders from him. Another rich blessing that comes from meditating on Christ's ownership of his church is to submit our agenda for revitalization completely to him, to his Word, to his Spirit. A great deal of the work of revitalization comes from sweeping away deep-rooted, man-centered agendas from previous generations that have become wild weeds choking out the life of the church. As Jesus said about false leaders in his day, "Every plant that my heavenly Father has not planted will be rooted up" (Matt. 15:13). So the work of revitalization must proceed by removing cherished false systems—traditions—of church life that the Father never planted: traditional Sunday school curriculum, worship patterns, church calendar commitments, partnerships, line items on the church budget, bylaws and personnel committee guidelines, uses for the building, and understandings of church government. These traditional aspects of church life come from human plans and commitments, not from Scripture. As the Lord said about ceremonial handwashing, "You leave the commandment of God and hold to the tradition of men" (Mark 7:8). Decades ago the church went astray because human leaders set aside God's Word for the sake of their ideas of church life.

No work of genuine revitalization can occur by a new generation of strong-willed leaders sweeping away old unscriptural, man-made traditions and replacing them with new traditions. Rather, these leaders must submit themselves first to Christ and like humble servants ask, "What do you want us to do?" They must diligently search the Scriptures for the best patterns of church ministry, all the while assuming the sufficiency of Scripture will lead them to a detailed, comprehensive understanding of church health. They must do so as humble servants of the King who want only to know his will and to do it. As the Lord said to Saul on the road to Damascus, "But rise and enter the city, and you will be told what you are to do" (Acts 9:6). Later Paul said, "I was not disobedient to the heavenly vision" (Acts 26:19). We should stand in the presence of King Jesus in reference to our specific local church and say, "What is your will? I will obey!"

This will help us avoid being authoritarian, self-promoting, and arrogant in our work of leading the church. Too many strong leaders have forgotten who they are and who Jesus is! Christ will use only truly humble servants who listen to his will to do the work of lasting revitalization. If you do not do that, you are scattering rather than gathering; you are deadening rather than revitalizing. You are just the next generation of a strong leader imposing his own agenda on a local church that is one step closer to having its lampstand removed.

This Is Something Only Christ Can Do, So Rest in Him

This work of revitalization is a supernatural work of sovereign grace. It is not merely the rescue of a building and a bank account, but it is fundamentally the transformation of human hearts. The people of God in that church had grown cold toward Christ; now, by God's grace, they are passionate for him once again. They had "abandoned the love you had at first" (Rev. 2:4), but now they have repented and done the things they did at first. They were "lukewarm" toward Christ, but instead of spewing them out of his mouth, the sovereign Lord sent forth his Spirit to make them hot for Christ again (Rev. 3:16). This change of human hearts is influenced by the Spirit of God through the Word of God, and it is done under the kingship of Jesus Christ. The exaltation of Christ over all things is the essence of this transformation. The theme of this chapter *is* the theme of the revitalization!

While there will be a great deal of labor, and undoubtedly the work of church revitalization will be physically, emotionally, mentally, and spiritually draining, in one sense we must "be still, and know" that Christ is Lord. He will be exalted in his church! (Ps. 46:10). We need to rest in the knowledge that he is powerfully active through his Spirit. We need to stand in Christ as our impenetrable fortress and know that no weapon forged against us will prevail, for he will refute every tongue that accuses us (Isa. 54:17).

PRACTICAL ADVICE

1. Be sure that Christ is supreme in your own heart, sovereign over the details of your life, ruling over your motives and plans for the church in all respects. Submit yourself daily to King Jesus in your quiet times, and throughout the day present your body to him as a living sacrifice (Rom. 12:1). You cannot lead in the framework of the sovereign kingship of Christ over his church if he does not have your allegiance.

2. Cry out to God daily in prayer that he would exalt his Son in your local church. In Psalm 110:1, God the Father says, "Sit at my right hand, until I make your enemies your footstool." The passion of God the Father for the glory of his Son is infinite, so unleash that zeal in prayer!

3. If you are a preacher or teacher of the Word, make certain that the absolute supremacy of Christ is clearly emphasized in all your teaching. Say often that Christ bought

55

the church with his blood; claim the church for Jesus like Columbus claimed Hispaniola for Queen Isabella—stick his banner in every beachhead where you wade ashore.

4. Submit all your plans for revitalization—the removal of old patterns and the establishment of new ones—to the Lord in prayer and to Scripture for review. Act like a servant, not a king, for Jesus himself is the King!

5. Draw great boldness and courage in revitalization from consistent meditation on the kingship of Jesus over your local church; let that meditation make human enemies shrink like the Anakites in Joshua's time (compare Num. 13:33 to Josh. 11:21–22—good-bye Anakites!).

6. Be a person after God's own heart. God is zealous for the glory of his Son, so you also must be.

7. Pray corporately, in the hearing of the whole church when possible, for Christ's kingship to be established plainly in your church.

8. Make certain that all your evangelism is Christ-centered and that converts have counted the cost and are ready to bow to King Jesus. This will revitalize your church powerfully.

9. Ask God to reveal the man-made plants that must be uprooted by the heavenly Father. Exalting Christ plainly should make those unscriptural traditions more evident and give you more strength to root them out.

10. Draw close to Christ as King to gain strength during times of persecution and slanderous attacks. Understand that the Lord stood at Paul's side and gave him strength (2 Tim. 4:17), and he will continue to protect his faithful servants.

11. Openly exalting Christ will protect you from taking credit if the Lord begins to bless your church with clear signs of revitalization. You will know that this has been a supernatural work of grace in the hearts of his people—and only King Jesus can do that.

12. Individual workers who are zealous for Christ's glory above all earthly glory cannot ultimately fail in revitalization, even if the church ultimately evicts them and eventually dies and the building becomes a fashion boutique or a mosque. He will not fail to reward faithful servants who suffer abuse for him, and some of his elect will be strengthened, even if they had lacked the power to change the final direction of the church.

13. Christ the King has promised to build his church, and the gates of hell will not prove stronger than it (Matt. 16:18). Continually appealing to the sovereign authority of Christ to do this will produce amazing perseverance within the hardest working servants.

14. Nominal Christians who populate dying churches do not like to talk about Jesus. At committee meetings, at church conferences, in the hallways, in sermons, in Bible studies, in worship, at corporate prayer, at all times— talk about Jesus a lot, especially his sovereign headship over that local church. Raise the spiritual temperature in the body so high that the spiritual viruses and bacteria will die or flee—and good health will result.[2] A vigorous establishment of Christ at the center of every aspect of church life is essential to the work of revitalization, so do it, and the church will be transformed.

4

Be Holy

No attribute of God is more vital for sinners to embrace than his holiness. This is clearly seen in the breathtaking encounter Isaiah had with the preincarnate Christ by whom he was called into prophetic service (Isa. 6). In the year that King Uzziah died, Isaiah saw the Lord—high and exalted. Above the Lord were seraphim calling to one another, "Holy, holy, holy is the LORD of hosts; the whole earth is full of his glory!" (Isa. 6:3). Scripture uses repetition for emphasis. Paul writes, "Rejoice in the Lord always; again I will say, rejoice" (Phil. 4:4). In Galatians 1:8–9, Paul repeats himself using the same exact words in successive verses: "If anyone is preaching to you a gospel contrary to the one you received, let him be accursed." Twenty-five times in the Gospel of John, Jesus underscored the importance of one of his statements by saying, "Truly, truly, I say to you." When he wanted to capture someone's full attention, he would repeat their name: "Simon, Simon, behold, Satan demanded to have you, that he might sift you like wheat" (Luke 22:31). Yet only once in all of Scripture is an attribute of God stated three times in a row: "Holy, holy, holy." We read twice in one chapter that "God is love" (1 John 4:8, 16), but we never read "God is love, love, love." Nor do we sinners read "God is grace, grace, grace," though we deeply need to fervently embrace both of these attributes. Therefore, in this awesome vision of Isaiah, with its triple assertion, "Holy, holy, holy," we have an eternal testimony to the primacy of God's holiness. How overpowering was the holiness of God to the seraphim who were covering their faces and feet! How full their hearts and how powerful their voices as they proclaimed this staggering truth! The doorposts and threshold of the temple shook at their voices, as though even inanimate creation trembles at the holiness of God. And if inanimate doorposts and thresholds shake at the sight of a thrice-holy God, how much more must we sinners tremble.

A Holy God

What does it mean that God is holy? The holiness of God has two aspects, and both of them are linked by the concept of *separation*. First, God is infinitely separate from all creation because he is the Creator and everything else is created. Second, God is infinitely separate from all evil, hating it with a perfect hatred and having absolutely nothing to do with it. Every human being should tremble in the presence of such a holy God for both of these reasons. All church revitalization efforts should delight in the fear of the Lord's holiness (Isa. 11:3) and derive purifying power from it (2 Cor. 11:2).

Perhaps the clearest indication of the first aspect of God's holiness—his infinite separation above all creation—is found in the same passage we have already seen, Isaiah 6. Why do the seraphim, who are perfectly free from all moral pollution and thus holy in that sense, cover their faces and feet before God's holiness? It cannot be from shame but, rather, from the awesome realization of how lofty this God is above them as their Creator. A. W. Tozer put it this way:

> Forever God stands apart, in light unapproachable. He is as high above an archangel as above a caterpillar, for the gulf that separates the archangel from the caterpillar is but finite, while the gulf between God and the archangel is infinite. The caterpillar and the archangel, though far removed from each other in the scale of created things, are nevertheless one in that they are alike created. They both belong in the category of that which-is-not-God and are separated from God by infinitude itself.[1]

Any church leader who desires to see his church revitalized must learn to melt inwardly in the presence of such a holy God, simply because of God's infinite majesty. Later in the book of Isaiah, God made plain the connection between the deep humility of reverence before God's holiness and the revival of both an individual and a church of such individuals: "For thus says the One who is high and lifted up, who inhabits eternity, whose name is Holy: 'I dwell in the high and holy place, and also with him who is of a contrite and lowly spirit, to revive the spirit of the lowly, and to revive the heart of the contrite'" (Isa. 57:15). God revitalizes any church that exudes such a spirit of deep reverence before his holiness.

As stated above, the second aspect of God's holiness is his infinite separation from all evil: "God is light, and in him is no darkness at all" (1 John 1:5). A direct implication of this is God's immeasurable zeal to purify his universe from all evil. When Scripture asserts that "God is a consuming fire" (Heb. 12:29), it is referring to God's commitment to incinerate all evil from his universe. In Scripture, fire either purifies or destroys. Both images are useful for us as sinners. Fire is seen as a purifier of precious metals taken as plunder in battle (Num. 31:22–23), and the same image is used for how the Lord will purify the Levites for his service (Mal. 3:2–3) and the remnant of believing Jews to worship his name (Zech. 13:9). For this reason Peter writes of our faith being purified as if by fire (1 Pet. 1:7). Sinners saved by grace should see themselves as standing in the consuming fire of God's holiness to be purified of sin until we are as morally pure as he is.

But the image of our holy God as a consuming fire also means wrath and judgment for the devil and his angels, as well as for all the sons of the devil who love and follow wickedness. Thus, the wicked city of Babylon will be consumed by fire as a judgment from an omnipotent and incensed God (Rev. 18:8). Hell is presented as a lake of fire into which all God's unholy enemies will be thrown (Rev. 19:20; 20:10; 21:8). And the second coming of Christ will result in the destruction of the universe by fire (2 Pet. 3:10, 12), purging all creation from the filth of wickedness.

All church revitalization must be done with a sense of the perfect hatred of almighty God toward sin. The zeal God has for a universe free from all moral darkness should be the driving power behind every sermon a revitalizing pastor preaches, every prayer a revitalizing church member prays, and every work a revitalizing strategist contemplates.

A Holy Savior

The image of Christ in Revelation 1 radiates with the holiness of God that we have already contemplated. Yet it becomes intensely personal for any Christian yearning to see their local church revitalized. Christ is dressed in a robe that reaches his feet, with a golden sash around his chest. His eyes are like blazing fire and his feet are like burnished bronze. Out of his mouth comes a sharp, double-edged sword. And his face is shining like the sun in its maximum brilliance (Rev. 1:13–16). This is a vision of a perfectly holy Priest-King who is actively moving through the seven golden lampstands.

In the letters to the seven churches, Christ uses the sword coming out of his mouth to judge the sin he sees with his eyes of blazing fire. For example, the church at Pergamum has some who hold to "the teaching of Balaam," resulting in idolatry and sexual immorality. Also at Pergamum are some who follow the teaching of the Nicolaitans, who seem to hold to a form of licentious and immoral pseudo-Christianity (Rev. 2:14–15). Hear the warning that Christ gives: "Therefore repent. If not, I will come to you soon and war against them with the sword of my mouth" (Rev. 2:16). Similarly, the church at Thyatira has a woman Christ calls "Jezebel," who misleads his people into sexual immorality and idolatry. Jesus threatens to strike her children (followers) dead: "And all the churches will know that I am he who searches mind and heart, and I will give to each of you according to your works" (Rev. 2:23). With his penetrating eyes of blazing fire, Jesus sees into the darkest recesses of every church member's heart, and especially of every leader. He removes the lampstands of churches that will not tremble at his holiness, and he fights against church members who refuse to fight against sin.

Like his Father, Jesus Christ "loved righteousness and hated wickedness" (Heb. 1:9). Both at the beginning and the end of his public ministry, Jesus took a whip and cleansed the temple. Zeal for his Father's house consumed him (John 2:17)—and still does to this day. Any church leader who desires to see his church revitalized must likewise delight in Christ's zeal to purify his own church from evil so that it will tremble with a holy awe at the infinite "otherness" of the almighty God.

A Holy Mission

The work of a church revitalizer is a subset of the general work of the gospel in the world, and the purpose of that gospel is to bring God glory by making sinners holy. Ephesians 1:4 says that God the Father chose the elect in Christ before the foundation of the world in order that we might be holy and blameless in his presence. To that end, he also ordained that the elect from every nation would be redeemed from the curse of the law by faith in the atoning work of Christ, transformed into increasing holiness by the power of the Spirit, and resurrected into glorious bodies free from every defilement of sin.

This is full salvation, and the gospel of Jesus Christ is the only power there is to effect salvation over all the earth (Rom. 1:16). The revitalization of a local church is done within the context of this greater work of holiness. So also the ordinary work of ministry in a healthy church is done with an eye to progressive growth in the holiness of its people. According to Romans 6:19, "For just as you once presented your members as slaves to impurity and to lawlessness leading to more lawlessness, so now present your members as slaves to righteousness leading to sanctification." The work of the gospel is in general a mighty work of holiness in the lives of people formerly enslaved by sin. As the gospel does its work, people are increasingly captivated by the majesty of the holiness of God as entirely and mysteriously "other," and they are increasingly filled with hatred for all wickedness both in their own lives and in the world. Revitalization is truly part of that greater work.

A Holy Church

The word translated *church* in the New Testament is from the Greek, meaning "called out." But called out from what? One passage in Revelation 18 answers that vital question. That chapter relates the fall of "Babylon the Great," a symbolic representation of the world in all its idolatrous and sensuous rebellion against God. It is a city and an empire dedicated to sexual immorality and overwhelming materialistic luxury (Rev. 18:3). It is the alluring whore who puts on the guise of enticement through her wares and delicacies, employing devious seductions to entice people all over the world to forsake God and live for the flesh. Babylon is the world's system that John warned against:

> Do not love the world or the things in the world. If anyone
> loves the world, the love of the Father is not in him. For all

that is in the world—the desires of the flesh and the desires of the eyes and pride of life—is not from the Father but is from the world. And the world is passing away along with its desires, but whoever does the will of God abides forever. (1 John 2:15–17)

James also offered his own warning: "You adulterous people! Do you not know that friendship with the world is enmity with God? Therefore whoever wishes to be a friend of the world makes himself an enemy of God" (James 4:4).

If, then, Babylon in Revelation 18 is the alluring world system, then the church is "called out" from her in Revelation 18:4–5: "Come out of her, my people, lest you take part in her sins, lest you share in her plagues; for her sins are heaped high as heaven, and God has remembered her iniquities." To "come out" of Satan's world by faith in Christ is to enter his church and be holy as he is holy. The true church is an assembly of people who, like Christ, hunger and thirst for righteousness (Matt. 5:6) and "have loved righteousness and hated wickedness" (Heb. 1:9).

Holiness, however, entails not only separation *from* evil but also separation *to the Lord* as his precious possession. The articles employed in the Old Testament sacrificial system were set apart as sacred—be it the priest himself (Exod. 28:36–38) or the atoning blood of the sacrifice (Exod. 30:10) or the incense (Exod. 30:37). The nation as a whole was called "holy to the LORD" (Deut. 7:6). The church is not merely to "come out from" Babylon; it must be "set apart unto the Lord" as his own. More than anything, it is the Word of God that sanctifies the church as separate from the world and holy to the Lord (John 17:17).

A healthy church will embrace both levels of God's holiness: first, they will have deep and abiding awe at God's infinite majesty; second, they will come out from "Babylon" and live pure and holy lives, putting sin to death by the Spirit. People who attend such a church will encounter the almighty God at their worship services—in the singing, praying, preaching, and fellowshipping. Just as Paul said of the Corinthian church, any outsider who comes into a worship service should hear clearly the Word expounded and cherished and be convinced that they are a sinner, having the secrets of their heart laid bare, and thus fall down and worship God, exclaiming, "God is really among you!" (1 Cor. 14:24–25).

It is precisely because a church has drifted from holiness that it needs to be revitalized. At some point, it ceased trembling at God's holiness, and its members began seeking to fill that emptiness with the idols of Babylon. They fell into secret patterns of sin. They began having conflicts with one another, as would carnal people. Their marriages began falling apart, sometimes because of adultery. They failed to raise their children in the nurture and admonition of the Lord. They busied themselves with the pursuit of money and other earthly goals. They became less discerning doctrinally and less passionate for biblical truth. They stopped reaching out with the gospel and started seeking the world's applause rather than the world's repentance. They forsook their first love and embraced the illicit love of the world. Ultimately, they began to wither and die. If one could take a spiritual "flight" through the secrets of the church members' hearts as Ezekiel did through the temple in Ezekiel 8, they would see modern versions of the abominations that provoked God to jealousy. A church does not die apart from a decisive move away from holiness. And revitalization begins with repentance for unholiness and a commitment to what God says: "You shall be holy, for I am holy" (1 Pet. 1:16).

A Holy Terror and a Holy Delight

How should a Christian see the holiness of God? Many who know almost nothing of it shrink back in disgust. They think of "holy people" as narrow-minded bigots who live out a strict morality based on arbitrary rules of austerity and who are almost completely defined by what they refuse to do, eat, say, and wear. Upon observing such "holiness" lived out by some eccentric groups, they reject holiness entirely. But this is a perversion of true biblical holiness. True holiness flows from encounters with the holy God by his Spirit and through his Word, and they are characterized by both *terror* and *pleasure.*

First, the encounter with God results in terror, as we see in Isaiah 6. The prophet, having such a vision of the holiness of Christ, was overwhelmed with his own smallness and sinfulness. He cried out, "Woe is me! For I am lost." John Calvin made this terror plain in his *Institutes of the Christian Religion*: "Hence that dread and amazement with which scripture uniformly relates holy men were struck and overwhelmed whenever they beheld the presence of God they are, in a manner, swallowed up and annihilated. Men are never duly touched and impressed with a conviction of their insignificance, until they have contrasted themselves with the majesty of God."[2] Church leaders and members alike begin to be revitalized when first they are overwhelmed with a sense of their sinfulness and smallness before such a holy God.

Second, the encounter with God also results in a greater sense of pleasure and pure moral beauty than we have ever experienced before. Psalm 29:2 commands us to worship the Lord "in the splendor of holiness." God's holiness is perfect beauty, with no admixture of corruption, no taint of poison, no whiff of decay. When the seraphim cried out that the "whole world is full of his glory" (Isa. 6:3), they saw God's beauty in everything he had ever done. The new heaven and new earth—perfectly free from evil—will be completely illuminated by the beauty of God's holiness. Jonathan Edwards captures this aspect of holiness as only he could:

> Holiness, as I then wrote down some of my contemplations on it, appeared to me to be of a sweet, pleasant, charming, serene, calm nature. It seemed to me it brought an inexpressible purity, brightness, peacefulness and ravishment to the soul: and that it made the soul like a field or garden of God, with all manner of pleasant flowers; that is all pleasant, delightful, and undisturbed: enjoying a sweet calm, and the gently vivifying beams of the sun. The soul of a true Christian, as I then wrote my meditations, appeared like such a little white flower as we see in the spring of the year; low and humble on the ground, opening its bosom to receive the pleasant beams of the sun's glory; rejoicing as it were in a calm rapture; diffusing around a sweet flagrancy; standing peacefully and lovingly, in the midst of other flowers round about; all in like manner opening their bosoms, to drink in the light of the sun.[3]

Holiness is sheer delight, radiant beauty, complete freedom from fear of judgment, irresistible attraction. Once the worshiper has tasted it, life is never the same. The battle against sin becomes driven by love, by a longing to taste again that sweet delight that only holiness can bring.

If a revitalizing pastor has felt the terror of God's holiness and the infinite humbling of God's lofty separation from all creation, and if he has also just as importantly tasted the almost indescribable delight of holiness, he will be best equipped as an instrument to lead his church. It will be a journey of a terror that protects—and a delight that allures.

PRACTICAL ADVICE

1. Whether you are a pastor or a church member who yearns to see the local church revitalized, you must begin with this: "Search me, O God, and know my heart! Try me and know my thoughts! And see if there be any grievous way in me, and lead me in the way everlasting" (Ps. 139:23–24). Ask God to reveal areas of sin in your own life. Repent and draw near to the holiness of God. Resolve to walk in the light as he is in the light (1 John 1:7).

2. Know that God does not require perfect holiness to be used by him to revitalize a church, for if he did, 1 John 1:7 would not link walking "in the light" with the promise that "the blood of Jesus his Son cleanses us from all sin." Ongoing purification from sin will be necessary as long as we are in this "body of death" (Rom. 7:24).

3. Pray that God will root out all sin from the hearts of the church members and that a standard of holiness will be so clearly erected in the ministry of the Word that the people will grow to hate their sins and love God's holiness.

4. Seek expressions of corporate worship, preaching, and prayer that display both the dread and perfect beauty of the Lord's holiness.

5. Expect that a higher standard of holiness in the general ministry of the church will arouse increasingly fierce opposition from people who will be unwilling to give up on their sins or their prideful false religion.

6. This higher standard of holiness will, in effect, increase the spiritual temperature in the church and drive out the infectious diseases or, conversely, it will result in the death of the church. Such a ministry will bring issues to a head, and people will no longer be able to remain complacent when faced with such a radiant display of the holiness of God. Consequently, all will be faced with the decision to either repent or drive away the people who espouse God's holiness.

7. Be certain as you advocate this holiness that you are not a hypocrite, nursing some private habitual sin of your own.[4]

8. Be certain to remember that all sinners are saved by grace—and that the blood of Christ has graciously covered your sins. This will make you sweetly humble while you vigorously oppose the sin that is harming the health of the church.

9. Pray that the church will eventually embrace biblical church discipline for the purpose of protecting itself from the leaven of sin that can spread through the whole lump if not purged out (1 Cor. 5:6).

5

Rely on God, Not on Yourself

God alone can give life, and God alone can revive a dying church. One of the greatest lessons for anyone yearning to see a church revitalized is to learn how to rely on God alone. What we may underestimate is how repugnant self-reliance is to God, how pervasive it is in us, how difficult it is to detect, and how stubborn it is to drive out. Identifying self-reliance in the work of church revitalization is an excellent starting point for the work God must do in his people, and especially in their leaders, before he will revive their spiritual lives.

Paul's Bitterest Lesson

The apostle Paul battled self-reliance his whole Christian life. It first expressed itself in the spiritual pride that characterized him before his conversion. Paul is the paradigm of someone who sought to establish his own righteousness before God by works of the law (Rom. 10:3; Gal. 1:14). He was fiercely proud of his Jewish credentials, as listed in Philippians 3:4–6, especially of his blamelessness in the law. This tendency to boast of his own achievements was revealed to be spiritual refuse (Phil. 3:8) in light of the glory of Christ that Paul first saw on the road to Damascus. But that does not mean that, at that instant, Paul was done with the astonishingly powerful gravitational pull of self-reliance.

In 2 Corinthians 1, Paul related the bitterest lesson of his life:

> For we do not want you to be unaware, brothers, of the affliction we experienced in Asia. For we were so utterly burdened beyond our strength that we despaired of life itself. Indeed, we felt that we had received the sentence of death. *But that was to make us rely not on ourselves but on God* who raises the dead. (2 Cor. 1:8–9; emphasis mine)

We do not know exactly what kind of hardship Paul was referring to; it surely had to do with some kind of persecution in connection with the ministry of the gospel. But Paul writes of God's purpose in orchestrating this overwhelming pressure on his soul: to teach him to stop relying on himself and, rather, to rely on God, who raises the dead. Paul still had some self-reliance deep within him, and only such a bitter affliction and a hopeless circumstance could begin to drive it out. Paul faced his own death, and he had no stratagems for delivering himself.

The Holy Spirit spoke this lesson to Paul's restless and fearful heart: "Stop relying on yourself; trust in God, who raises the dead. That is the ultimate issue in salvation, for death is the final enemy. And, Paul, what is your strategy for raising your own corpse from the grave? What power will you summon? What argument will you make? What bribe can you pay? All means will be gone. God will raise you from the dead, or you will never be raised. So, if that be true, dear Paul, why not trust him now for deliverance from this extreme (but lesser) trial? Drive out self-reliance with faith."

Now, if a godly man like Paul needed this level of instruction on the issue of self-reliance, how much more do we need it? Paul's powerful summation of his lesson came with the words, "On him we have set our hope" (2 Cor. 1:10). Setting your hope on God is the opposite of self-reliance. This is directly related to church revitalization, for what is revitalization but the supernatural work of God in raising a church from the dead? If you approach church revitalization looking at your own strength—your wisdom, technique, verbal skills, reasoning, winsome personality, people skills, shrewdness, or even revitalization experience at some other church—you are being self-reliant. On God, and God alone, you must set your hope.

Arrogance and Despair: Two Sides of the Same Coin

Self-reliance is so deeply rooted that it may be very difficult to detect—and hard to eradicate once detected. One of the greatest ways to expose this enemy of God's glory is to gauge your heart when you look at the challenges you face in revitalization. Zeal for God's glory has been reduced to a mere flicker, numbers have dwindled, finances are diminishing, nominal Christians are in control with their worldly outlook, evangelism has been nonexistent for years, and the future looks dim. On top of all that, some church members are vocal in their opposition to clear, biblical preaching, while the stench of hidden sin is wafting through their lives. These, and many other obstacles, face you as you look down the road ahead.

If at that moment you feel overwhelming despair, you are indulging in self-reliance. However, if you feel a surging confidence in what you will be able to achieve by your gifts and persuasiveness and are looking forward to the challenge as an opportunity to "show what you can do," you are also indulging in self-reliance. Despair and arrogance are two sides of the same coin—and that coin is called self-reliance.

We see this most plainly in the tragic events recounted by Moses in Deuteronomy 1. Forty years earlier, Moses had sent out some spies to scout the land, yet they returned with the spiritual virus of unbelief. They caught it while gazing at the walled cities and the warriors they would have to defeat to conquer the land. "The people are greater and taller than we. The cities are great and fortified up to heaven" (Deut. 1:28). "We seemed to ourselves like grasshoppers, and so we seemed to them" (Num. 13:33). They looked at the challenges facing them, which were real indeed, but then made the spiritually fatal mistake of looking *inward* to meet these challenges. When they looked inward and did not see the resources necessary, they melted in despair.

But God was angry at their wretched unbelief in forgetting all the power he had shown in delivering them from Egypt and the Red Sea. And he swore on oath that they would never inherit the land, condemning them to wander for forty years in the desert until their children would rise up to inherit it in their place. At that point they changed their minds, and each of them prepared for battle, thinking "it easy to go up into the hill country" (Deut. 1:41). This was nothing more than the exact same thing—self-reliance—in its opposite guise of arrogance. And God willed that the Amorites who lived in the hill country should drive them out like a swarm of bees (Deut. 1:44).

Church revitalization is one of the most difficult works on which a Christian can ever embark. No one is harder to reach than an unconverted church member. They have resisted biblical instruction their entire lives and are veteran "opposers" to God's work. Concerning pastors, they have "seen 'em come and seen 'em go." As a matter of fact, some of them have been instrumental in making them go! They consider the church to be theirs, and they will fight you every step of the way. Others are not so belligerent, but they are usually listless, lethargic, and lifeless. Amid all this may be a godly remnant who have wept and prayed for years for revival, but with no apparent success. They are discouraged and growing weaker.

When a new leader surveys such a scene, it is tempting to look inward for the resources to meet these challenges. If such a leader does look inward and (most likely) does not see those resources—courage, boldness, perseverance, wisdom, persuasiveness, people skills, and the like—he will be overwhelmed with discouragement. This is a sure sign of self-reliance. On the flip side, self-reliance can produce false confidence as a leader looks inward and somehow sees the necessary resources. In fact, the same leader may do each of these at different times in the journey of church revitalization.

75

Sometimes downcast, sometimes pridefully elated, depending on the circumstances. Beware! This is self-reliance—the ancient enemy of God's glory.

PRACTICAL ADVICE

1. Meditate on 2 Corinthians 1:8–11, and grow in your sense of the pervasive danger of self-reliance. Ask God to use the trials that inevitably come with church revitalization to teach you to no longer rely on yourself but on God. God raises dead people—and dead churches!

2. Ask God in prayer to show you patterns of self-reliance. Ask him to expose moments of arrogance on the one side, or despair on the other. When you are feeling either one, repent and ask for God's forgiveness.

3. As you gather other church members to join revitalization efforts, make prayer a centerpiece in the battle against self-reliance. Nothing destroys self-reliance as much as prayer and the ministry of the Word.

4. If you are a regular preacher or teacher of the Word, speak often about church growth and revitalization as something only God can do.

5. As the church begins to make some progress, give God all the glory both in your heart and in public. Express thanks to God for the little victories along the way. This will heighten your sense of reliance on God.

6. Look to Christ as the vine and the members as branches (John 15:5), and intensify your sense of reliance on Christ as the only source of life and health for the church.

7. Memorize these verses: "I planted, Apollos watered, but God gave it growth. So neither he who plants nor he who waters is anything, but only God who gives the growth" (1 Cor. 3:6–7). Say to yourself based on these words, "I am nothing; God is everything!"

8. Identify all moments of despair as self-reliance. Read the later chapter in this book on discouragement (chapter 13) in light of this lesson. Repent from all forms of despair.

9. Think and speak often of church revitalization as something God does "to the praise of his glory" (Eph. 1:12, 14). Understand that all self-reliance deprives God of his glory.

10. Consider the revitalization of your church a miracle of God's grace. Pray for the miracle to happen. Say often, "If God wills, this church will flourish!"

11. Trust in God's promises for the health of your walk with Christ, as well as the walk of others. Be filled with good hope that God will be glorified in every faithful effort: "Knowing that in the Lord your labor is not in vain" (1 Cor. 15:58).

6

Rely on God's Word, Not on Techniques

The powerful Word of God has been building Christ's kingdom since the beginning of redemptive history. It has never been defeated, and it never will be. Satan has been opposing God's Word since he slithered up to Eve in the Garden of Eden and questioned God's authority, recruiting humanity through Adam to join his rebellion. But since that dreadful moment, God's Word has been destroying Satan's kingdom, pushing back the darkness and rescuing the elect captives. Satan has never been able to tame the Word, to chain the Word, to stop the Word, or to make the Word extinct. And the Word of God alone will revitalize a church if it is to be revitalized. The more the revitalizing leaders trust the Word of God alone, the more powerful their efforts will be.

Revitalization Comes by Hearing

Revitalization is nothing less than the transformation of individual human hearts—by either conversion or sanctification—on a church-wide scale. This work of comprehensive salvation from sin comes only through faith in Jesus Christ, and Romans 10:17 says saving faith comes by hearing the Word. It doesn't matter what other things happen in your church; if the Word of God is not central to the revitalization effort, no genuine transformation will ever occur. The church has come to need revitalization because its leaders and members have turned away from God through sin, resulting in spiritual deadness. The Word of God in its testimony to the saving work of Christ is the only method given to churches by which they can be revitalized.

Perhaps the clearest verse in the Bible on the essence of regeneration is 2 Corinthians 4:6: "For God, who said, 'Let light shine out of darkness,' has shone in our hearts to give the light of the knowledge of the glory of God in the face of Jesus Christ." This is the miracle of regeneration, of being made a new creation in Christ. Paul likens the power of God to speak life into a dead soul to the power he displayed at creation in speaking light into a dark universe. This moment of spiritual creation is the basic "building block" of any church revitalization effort. A subsequent work is like it: the increasing illumination in the hearts of existing regenerate church members by the Spirit of God. This progressive work of illumination reveals God's radiant glory in Christ, as well as God's purposes for our lives and for his church. Faith is, as I will make plain in chapter 8, the eyesight of the soul (Matt. 6:22) by which we can see invisible realities, including the way the local church is falling short of God's plan. Revitalization occurs when the Word of God is clearly unfolded before their very eyes. No other power or invention of human contrivance can bring about these changes in the human heart. Revitalization comes by hearing God's Word.

Therefore, the centerpiece of the ministry of the Word of God in the pulpit, in Sunday school, and in all Bible studies and discipleship relationships must be the clear proclamation of Christ crucified and resurrected as the only Savior for sinners. Though the ongoing preaching of lesser doctrines is also essential to a complete ministry of the Word, the gospel of Christ must be paramount. As Paul said, "And I, when I came to you, brothers, did not come proclaiming to you the testimony of God with lofty speech or wisdom. For I decided to know nothing among you except Jesus Christ and him crucified" (1 Cor. 2:1–2). Here, Paul is rejecting the human wisdom that was the glory of Greece and the envy of the pagan world of his time. The wisdom of God for the sinful human race is the cross of Christ. Lift it high!

The Sufficiency of Scripture and FBC Durham

Peter asserted, "His divine power has granted to us all things that pertain to life and godliness, through the knowledge of him who called us to his own glory and excellence, by which he has granted to us his precious and very great promises, so that through them you may become partakers of the divine nature, having escaped from the corruption that is in the world because of sinful desire" (2 Pet. 1:3–4). God's Word is fully sufficient to enable us to be conformed to Christ and escape the corruption of sin. Every church revitalizer should "put all his eggs in one basket" by putting his full trust in God's Word to prosper his efforts at transforming the church. As Psalm 1 says, "Blessed is the man who walks not in the counsel of the wicked, nor stands in the way of sinners, nor sits in the seat of scoffers; but his delight is in the law of the LORD, and on his law he meditates day and night. He is like a tree planted by streams of water that yields its fruit in its season, and its leaf does not wither. *In all that he does, he prospers*" (vv. 1–3; emphasis mine). What a promise! God will prosper any servant of the Lord who fully invests their heart in God's Word.

The sufficiency of Scripture to make FBC healthy and glorifying to God has been the central pillar of my ministry since I was being interviewed for the position of senior pastor of FBC back in August 1998. During the interview, I sat in the parlor of our church and was quizzed on various aspects of church ministry by the seven members of the search committee. I had with me my pocket Bible, and as they asked one question after another about church life, I kept opening the Bible to this or that passage and answered based on the texts that I felt the Holy Spirit was bringing to my mind. As the interview wore on and I continued to do this, one of the committee members began to laugh and said, "You really believe all the answers are in that book, don't you?" I answered, "For the life and fruitfulness of a local church, yes I do!" Her amazement and mirth were not unfriendly, but they were also warning signs as to the journey of revitalization on which I was about to embark. The idea of the sufficiency of Scripture for the full fruitfulness of any local church is, if anything, even stronger in my mind today than it was then.

To deny the sufficiency of Scripture to build the church of Jesus Christ is to imply that some other human technique or methodology is necessary to supplement the Word of God. And that cannot be.

Many at FBC were strongly opposed to a faithful, biblical ministry. Their disdain of the God of the Bible became apparent at key moments. This will be common in many church revitalization situations. The teaching of the Bible, especially in the ways that most clearly run counter to the prevailing notions of the surrounding secular culture, will seem foreign to them. For me, the issue that I had to address at FBC was that of "gender and authority," or the fact that God has ordained male leadership in the Bible. This stands in stark contrast to the feminist and egalitarian notions prevalent in our culture. As I began teaching and leading on this issue, many in the church were deeply offended and began to rise up in opposition.

I worked with our deacons (the lay leaders of the church at that time) to lay a biblical foundation for these convictions. We had a Saturday teaching time that was greatly irksome to many of them. For that session, I had written a thirty-page paper titled "Gender and Authority in the Church" and presented it to them. It was one of the worst meetings I have ever attended. I went step by step through the document, describing first the authority of God in the universe, how God delegates that authority to created beings and gives them laws by which they are to exercise their authority, how God will call each leader to account for his leadership, how Christ serves as a clear example of servant-leadership, and how God established male leadership in the home and in the church. We went through key passages like 1 Timothy 2;

Galatians 3; Ephesians 5; 1 Corinthians 11 and 14; and so forth. It became clear at that point how divided our church was. Some of the deacons were truly delighted in the clear teaching of Scripture. Others were aghast and enraged.

I remember well the most powerful leader of the faction that was most threatening the church and the horrible look on his face as I was teaching. At one point, I was asserting that God has prescribed in Scripture how the church is to be run and that we have no right to seize hold of the church and do it our own way. I used the story of David bringing the ark of the covenant to Jerusalem on an oxcart (contrary to the laws of Moses), and when the oxen stumbled, Uzzah grabbed hold of the ark to stabilize it. When the Bible declared that God struck Uzzah dead for his irreverent act, this deacon recoiled physically in his chair and was appalled. He gestured down at the open Bible on the table before him and said, "I could never believe in a God like that!" That moment crystallized the need for reform at FBC. This man could not believe in the God who is clearly revealed in the pages of the Bible lying open on the table in front of him. What God could he believe in then? One of his own imagination, it seems; one who would never kill people out of holy indignation at the violation of his laws; one who certainly would never send any "good person" to hell for an eternity. His god was a reasonable god that made sense to him—an idol.

That Saturday morning was an abomination to many of those deacons. They wanted a church that was socially comfortable, a pleasant place of barbecues, family gatherings, and entertaining messages about God's love. Others were more aggressive in their opposition, saying to me, "Where does your authority come from to tell a woman she may not run for deacon? Who do you think you are?" For them, it was an issue of power and control. Still, some were more pragmatic in their arguments and less confrontational, but no more motivated by scriptural truth than the others. Then there were some who were delighted in the faithful teaching of the Word of God.

At many meetings after that, I came face-to-face with the deep antipathy many of the church members had to more controversial aspects of God's Word. At one point, one woman said, "I don't give a flip what Paul thought about this!" She was willing to throw out the apostle's teachings if it did not agree with what she thought was right. Another time at a prayer meeting, a woman prayed, "Lord, help us to realize that we are a modern people, and we do not need to do whatever the Bible says." One godly member of the church later said it should be included in a top-ten list of "Prayers Least Likely to Be Answered by God." As I continued to preach chapter after chapter of the Bible from the pulpit on Sundays—not using the pulpit to voice my personal opinions on the growing controversy but simply seeking to feed the sheep and preach the gospel to the lost—the church was being revitalized before our eyes.

Sola Scriptura and Luther's "Laziness"

The phrase "the sufficiency of Scripture" is merely a modern English way of referring to one of the five central pillars of the Protestant Reformation of the sixteenth and seventeenth centuries, *sola scriptura*: "by Scripture alone." Martin Luther, the leader of the German Reformation, began his spiritual pilgrimage for salvation from God's wrath by joining an Augustinian monastery in 1505. Yet no matter how hard he worked, his conscience was always there to accuse him of his latent sins. He was about to drive himself insane with all his efforts for inner peace. But God, in his rich mercy, illuminated one key passage of Scripture: "For in it the righteousness of God is revealed from faith for faith, as it is written, 'The righteous shall live by faith'" (Rom. 1:17). Luther pondered this text and began to realize that the "righteousness of God" in that verse was good news for sinners, because it explained the gospel as the "power of God for salvation to everyone who believes" (Rom. 1:16).

> Then I grasped that the justice of God is that righteousness by which through grace and sheer mercy God justifies us through faith. Thereupon I felt myself to be reborn and to have gone through open doors into paradise. The whole of scripture took on a new meaning, and whereas before the "justice of God" had filled me with hate, now it became to me inexpressibly sweet in greater love. This passage of Paul became to me a gate to heaven.[1]

For Luther, the liberation of saving faith in Christ came only from Scripture, not from the Roman Catholic Church's elaborate system of religious works. At that time, all spiritual truth was mediated to the people by the Roman Catholic hierarchy. No individual church member had direct access to the Word of God, and all the speaking done in the mass was done in Latin, which most of the common people of Germany could not understand. The Protestant Reformation cut through all this, with Luther boldly leading the way. Luther's courage in standing alone, his life in peril, against all this human power and human tradition represents the main idea of our faith—the responsibility of every individual to make a wise decision for their own soul and to trust in Christ based on God's Word alone, not on human inventions.

At his trial for heresy at the Diet of Worms in 1521, Luther made this powerful assertion: "Unless I am convinced by scripture and plain reason—I do not accept the authority of the popes and councils, for they have contradicted each other—my conscience is captive to the Word of God. I cannot and I will not recant anything for to go against conscience is neither right nor safe. God help me. Amen."[2] Luther staked his life and his soul on the Word of God.

Luther lived the rest of his life to spread the Word of God to everyone he could. God's Word, unleashed by his and others' efforts, resulted in a transformed German church and the salvation of countless millions around the world. This was the principle of *sola scriptura*: by the Scripture alone can a sinner find Christ and be saved for all eternity. How vital it is for modern church reformers (revitalizers) to remember this principle! In a sermon in 1522, Luther gave this humorous account of his "lazy" efforts at reformation:

> I simply taught, preached, wrote God's Word; otherwise I did nothing. And then, while I slept, or drank Wittenberg beer with my Philip and my Amsdorf, the Word so greatly weakened the papacy that never a prince or emperor did such damage to it. I did nothing. The Word did it all.[3]

This same trust in the Bible's power to change hearts must drive all healthy efforts at church revitalization in our age as well.

The Word *Alone* versus the "Science" of Revitalization

We are fighting here the spirit of Charles Finney and his commitment to technique and the "science" of revival. The basic idea is that if you do the work properly, you will of necessity get a revival every time. He writes, "A revival of religion is not a miracle, nor dependent on a miracle in any sense. It is a purely philosophical result of the right use of the constituted means—as much so as any other effect produced by the application of means."[4] The "application of means" Finney developed came to be called his "new measures," and this became the prototype for modern evangelicalism's faith in technique over the Word of God.[5] One of Finney's critics at the time, Princeton professor Albert Dod, declared that through Finney's "experiments with the efficacy of different measures, the house of God becomes transformed into a kind of laboratory."[6]

The idea that revival—or for our purposes, revitalization—can be reduced to a series of inevitably successful principles or techniques is still alive today. All you have to do is Google something like "ten easy steps to church renewal," and you will get an amazing potpourri of practical advice. That is the danger of a book like this one as well. Every church revitalization situation is unique, with its own set of challenges. Yet in every case, true revitalization comes not with man-developed techniques, but with a firm reliance on the sufficiency of the Word of God to transform human hearts.

In the twenty-first century, man-centered revitalization techniques focus on other ways to tickle the sensibilities of seekers, attenders, and church members. These techniques are not much different than the approach of the medieval

Roman Catholic Church or that of Finney and the other preachers of the Second Great Awakening. The appeal to the five senses in the Middle Ages resulted in amazing cathedrals with soaring architecture, stunning stained glass windows, magnificent sculptures, the majestic tones of pipe organs, and the "smells and bells" of the Latin mass. The appeal to the senses in Finney's era centered on a style of preaching that employed high volume and energy in theatrical presentations of biblical themes, the psychological pressure made by the "anxious bench" (later developed into the techniques of the "invitation" and the "altar call"), and the use of culturally pleasing frontier music. Our techniques might include a sleek-looking building designed to look like a country club, state-of-the-art electronics, cutting-edge worship music that stays current with popular tastes, the use of handheld smartphones and Twitter accounts to enable an interactive connection with the preacher and the audience, and "relevant" sermons that immediately address felt needs of the hearers and stay away from deep theology. The employment of such human-centered techniques will never produce genuine transformation of the human heart and, therefore, will never produce genuine revitalization.

The Pulpit: The Word Alone Unleashed a Line at a Time

The most significant force in the revitalization of any local church is the ongoing ministry of the Word of God from the pulpit Sunday after Sunday. If you are a revitalizing church member, you need to pray that God will raise up a faithful biblical expositor to preach God's Word from the pulpit of your church. If that is already happening, you must pray that God will sustain that man in his difficult work, for there often comes a time in church revitalization when the unregenerate church members "will not endure sound teaching" but will seek to gather around themselves teachers to say what their itching ears long to hear (2 Tim. 4:3). To do this, they must get rid of this irksome preacher who is offending them with powerfully convicting words of truth.

If you are the man God has raised up to preach week after week from the pulpit of a church, your calling is to be faithful to him by accurately preaching his Word. As John MacArthur's "Grace to You" ministry puts it, "Unleashing God's Word one verse at a time."[7] I believe that expositional preaching is by far the most effective and powerful form of preaching in the revitalization of a church. By expositional, I mean that the main point of the sermon is the main point of the text being preached. I would also say that the consecutive preaching of line upon line and chapter upon chapter and book upon book can be used by God to build a foundation of solid doctrine that will enable the church to flourish for generations to come. However, a topical sermon that the preacher selects according to what he feels best suits the moment can lead to some difficulties. For example, in writing the sermon, the pastor may come to the text with a preconceived notion of what he wants to say, and it is easier to take the passage out of context. It is also more likely that such a topical approach to preaching may result in the pastor riding certain hobbyhorses.

Paul said to the Ephesian elders, "I did not shrink from declaring to you anything that was profitable, and teaching you in public and from house to house" (Acts 20:20), and

"I did not shrink from declaring to you the whole counsel of God" (v. 27). In chapter 10 on courage, we will discuss the notion of "shrinking back" from texts of Scripture, but it is worth mentioning here that Paul makes it plain that he desired to unfold the "whole counsel of God" and "anything that was profitable" (which is all Scripture, not just some of it; see 2 Tim. 3:16). Gain the people's trust by faithfully handling the Word of God. When they trust you, the church as a whole will be less likely to divide regarding difficult doctrines.

PRACTICAL ADVICE

1. Look to your own heart and life first. Are you having a daily quiet time in the Word? Are you feeding your soul daily on the Word of God? "Man shall not live on bread alone, but by every word that comes from the mouth of God" (Matt. 4:4).

2. Memorize Scripture, even whole books of the Bible. This will be a powerful tool in transforming your own heart and equipping you to minister to others. And if you are a regular preaching pastor in a local church, the time you invest in memorization will pay back dividends that you can scarcely imagine in all aspects of your ministry, but especially your preaching ministry.

3. Trust in the Word of God to revitalize your church. Put all your eggs in this one basket. Look again at the promise in Psalm 1:1–3 that you will prosper in whatever you do. This especially applies to the blessing of God's people in a local church.

4. Reject human techniques and transferable concepts that are "guaranteed" to work in every church. Trust in the Word to do the work.

5. If you are a regular preacher of the Word, embrace expositional preaching as the centerpiece of your ministry. Seek to feed Christ's sheep faithfully with nothing but the Word of God. Understand that the work of revitalization is a subset of the gospel ministry of reconciliation of sinners to God through the gospel of Jesus Christ. Make certain that the main point of your sermon is always the main point of the text. Stand humbly under the Word of God and faithfully deliver what it says to the people. Avoid hobbyhorses and selected texts that you are tempted to "hurl" at particularly irksome opponents. That is a misuse of the pulpit.

6. If you are a preacher, then consider sequential exposition of books of the Bible. Think about how you may best work in "unleashing God's Word one verse at a time." Choose books that will maximally educate the church members early on in your revitalization effort without causing them to stumble over doctrines for which they are not yet ready. Perhaps start with a simple gospel epistle like 2 Timothy or Philippians. Then move gradually to weightier books like Romans, Ephesians, or Galatians. Build trust patiently.

7. If you are a lay leader, not a preacher, pray for these things for your pastor.

8. Be confident in the power of God's Word. Never be ashamed of anything the Word teaches. Know that unregenerate church members will stumble badly over the

more controversial aspects of the Word and will blame you as though you wrote them. Deal with such ignorance patiently and faithfully, proving your doctrines carefully from texts of Scripture.

9. Teach the congregation the value of the ministry of the Word. If you are a pastor, make Bible study your top priority. Give yourself faithfully to developing as a preacher. Paul said this to Timothy: "Practice these things, immerse yourself in them, so that all may see your progress. Keep a close watch on yourself and on the teaching. Persist in this, for by so doing you will save both yourself and your hearers" (1 Tim. 4:15–16). Understand that the ongoing work of salvation (both in your soul and in the soul of your hearers) depends on your faithful ministry of the Word.

10. In church revitalization situations, people's immaturity concerning the Word of God can be appalling. Perhaps the church has not had faithful preaching or teaching in years. Be patient and persevere.

11. Read books on church growth, health, revitalization, and revival. Do so knowing that there is no transferable formula for success that will work every time. Be skeptical of techniques that do not make central the sovereign power of God.

7

Saturate the Church in Prayer

One difficult day, Jesus had to confront his humbled disciples after they had failed miserably. Jesus had been up on a mountain with three of his apostles. A man had brought his demon-possessed boy to the remaining nine apostles, but they could not drive out the demon. When Jesus came down from the mountaintop and found out what had happened, he exclaimed, "O faithless generation, how long am I to be with you? How long am I to bear with you? Bring him to me" (Mark 9:19). Jesus then drove out the demon in a great display of his power. Later, the apostles came to Jesus privately and asked, "Why could we not cast it out?" Jesus answered most poignantly, "This kind cannot be driven out by anything but prayer" (Mark 9:28–29).

The convicting insight came as I realized the significance of what Jesus said. *These men had not prayed!* They had sought to do a miracle in their own strength. Perhaps they had remembered their earlier successes in driving out demons and felt they had the technique down. But their prayerless attempt showed a self-reliance that is repugnant to God. Jesus said, "Apart from me you can do nothing" (John 15:5). Is there any demon a human being can drive out apart from the power of God? Is there a successful, godless technique for a miracle? The apostles' prayerlessness displayed a root of pride and self-sufficiency. Just as no demon comes out except by prayer, no church can be revitalized except by prayer.

Church revitalization will only ever happen in answer to faith-filled, prevailing prayer. It is greatly to the glory of God to revitalize a church of humble, prayerful people. But it is greatly dishonoring to him to suppose this transformation can come about any other way.

Christ's Church: Birthed in Prayer, Renewed in Prayer

The church of Jesus Christ was birthed as a world-changing force at a prayer meeting. In that upper room in Jerusalem on the day of Pentecost, as the small group of disciples was gathered to pray continually and wait on God to send the gift of the promised Holy Spirit (Acts 1:4–5, 14), suddenly there came the sound of a rushing wind and the appearance of tongues of fire. They were all filled with the Holy Spirit and began speaking in tongues as the Spirit enabled them (Acts 2:1–4). There was a great ingathering of souls that day by the power of sovereign grace: three thousand were added to their number. It is no accident that humble, united, prevailing, patient prayer preceded the outpouring of the Spirit and the harvest of souls into the church. When the church forsakes this kind of prayer, it takes a vigorous step toward its own extinction.

Seeing such corporate prayer again and again in the book of Acts shows how lasting this paradigm was intended to be. The filling of the Spirit was not "once for all." In this way, it is wonderfully different from the atoning work of Jesus Christ on the cross, which was clearly once for all (see especially Heb. 9:26–28). So in Acts 4:23–31, after Peter and John had been arrested for performing a miraculous healing at the temple and were threatened with grave punishments if they continued to preach the gospel, the men returned to the church, and all those gathered poured out their hearts in a Bible-saturated, faith-filled, urgent prayer for boldness. God's awesome response confirms my assertion that the supernaturally powerful prayer meeting on the day of Pentecost was not once for all but meant to be reenacted again and again: "When they had prayed, the place in which they were gathered together was shaken, and they were all filled with the Holy Spirit and continued to speak the word of God with boldness" (Acts 4:31). A key insight is that this was *not exactly like Pentecost*, but it was *essentially like Pentecost*. The power of God was poured out on the church in an amazing way, enabling it to be filled with the Spirit and speak God's Word boldly. Internal transformation resulted in evangelistic fruitfulness. We see the same pattern in Acts 13, when the church in Antioch was united in prayer and the Holy Spirit said, "Set apart for me Barnabas and Saul for the work to which I have called them" (v. 2). After the church had fasted and prayed, they sent these missionaries out to change the Gentile world (Acts 13–14).

I am commending this insight to you as a church revitalizer. Assemble like-minded people in your church and ask God to pour out his Spirit on you, filling you with his Spirit, displaying the fruit of the Spirit (Gal. 5:22–23) in you, empowering you to speak God's Word boldly, transforming people's hearts, and changing the world.

Prayer and the History of Revival

Throughout church history, the pattern I have asserted from Acts 2, 4, and 13 has been reenacted. God has answered extraordinary corporate prayer for his renewing work by pouring out his Holy Spirit on his people, resulting in deep conviction of sin and assurance of salvation. This has resulted in the transformed church being empowered to change the world through evangelism and benevolence ministries. A. T. Pierson said, "There has never been a spiritual awakening in any country or locality that did not begin in united prayer."[1] Before him, Matthew Henry said, "When God intends great mercy for his people, he first sets them praying."[2] Jonathan Edwards similarly asserted, "It is the manner of God, before he bestows any signal mercy on the people, first to prepare them for it; and before he removes any awful judgments which he hath brought upon them for their sins, first to cause them to forsake those sins which procured those judgments."[3] So in the matter of revitalization, when God is determining to renew a church from a cold, backslidden, unbelieving state, he first prepares them for it through prayer, causing them to forsake their sinful self-sufficiency and worldliness and to seek his face with great fervor. In some ways, we could argue that churches do not merely pray for revival but that prayer itself *is* the revival.

History recounts many thrilling answers to extraordinary, united prayer for revival. For example, on January 1, 1734, John Wesley wrote these words in his journal:

> In Fetter Lane with about sixty of our brethren. About three in the morning as we were continuing instant in prayer the power of God came mightily upon us, insomuch that many cried out for exulting joy and many fell to the ground. As soon as we were recovered a little from the awe and amazement at the presence of His Majesty, we broke out with one voice, "We praise Thee, O God, we acknowledge Thee to be the Lord."[4]

The revitalization of your local church in answer to prayer may well add to this amazing historical record of the works of God!

Prayer: Scripture's Commands and Promises

Far more important than historical accounts, however, are the many commands and promises in Scripture connected with prayer. Jesus said,

> And I tell you, ask, and it will be given to you; seek, and you will find; knock, and it will be opened to you. For everyone who asks receives, and the one who seeks finds, and to the one who knocks it will be opened. What father among you, if his son asks for a fish, will instead of a fish give him a serpent; or if he asks for an egg, will give him a scorpion? If you then, who are evil, know how to give good gifts to your children, how much more will the heavenly Father give the Holy Spirit to those who ask him! (Luke 11:9–13)

Notice that Jesus said "the heavenly Father" will give "the Holy Spirit" to those who ask him. Looking at this now, post-Pentecost, we can see this as a fresh effusion of the Holy Spirit poured out on us who already have received the Spirit but who yearn for greater displays of the fruit of the Spirit, power in the Spirit for holiness and mortification of sin (Rom. 8:13), a stronger sense of assurance of our salvation (v. 16), and greater power and boldness in evangelism (Acts 1:8; 4:31).

The apostle John gave us this promise: "This is the confidence that we have toward him, that if we ask anything according to his will he hears us. And if we know that he hears us in whatever we ask, we know that we have the requests that we have asked of him" (1 John 5:14–15). Take that promise and "show it to God." Thomas Manton spoke of praying back the promises of God in this way: "Show him his writing; God is tender of his word."[5] As you pray Scripture back to God, do so with amazing persistence and zeal, like the persistent widow of Luke 18:1–5. God tests the sincerity of our zeal for church reform by making us wait for answers. I do not believe we should try to force God's hand by "tarrying meetings" in which we stay in one room until God pours out his Spirit. God may make the church wait for many weeks, months, or even years. But we should come back to focused corporate prayer for renewal again and again until God revitalizes the church.

The Mystery of Prayer

Spirit-led prayer has two effects, and both of them are essential to church revitalization. The first is reasonable; the second is mysterious. First, prayer changes us. Second, prayer changes things. It makes perfect sense to us that prayer changes the hearts of all who invest themselves passionately in it. Prayer conforms us to God's heart and plans and makes us long for them to be consummated. When we pray, we are turning our backs on the Laodicean lukewarmness (Rev. 3:16) that is of the essence of a church that needs revitalization. When we pray, we are remembering the height from which we have fallen, we are repenting of having forsaken our first love like the Ephesian church, and we are doing the things we did at the beginning of our Christian lives to display our love for Christ (Rev. 2:5). In this way, we are pleading for Christ to not come and remove our lampstand. All of this makes perfect sense—the more we invest in our prayers, the more committed to God's purposes we will become, simply because we have sacrificed our time and brought forth our hearts to be touched. The more the people of a church pray, the more revitalized the church will become.

I would compare the effect of prayer on our hearts to a blacksmith's bellows and coals heating up a cold, black piece of iron, rendering it red-hot, ready to be pounded on the anvil by the craftsman:

> Prayer is the furnace, the coal bed by which our hearts are heated up from their black coldness toward the things of God to desire what we didn't care about before: his pleasure, his presence, his face, his glory, the salvation of lost people, relief for the poor, improvement in marriages, establishment of fruitful ministries.[6]

But prayer is also infinitely mysterious. The well-known slogan "Prayer changes things" becomes more mysterious the more you understand the meticulous nature of God's sovereign plan. Ephesians 1:11 says that God "works all things according to the counsel of his will." God's plan includes the greatest of issues (the rise and fall of nations; see Isaiah 14:26) and the smallest of details (like sparrows dying; see Matt. 10:29). God makes it plain that he accepts no counsel or advice from man: "Whom did he consult, and who made him understand? Who taught him the path of justice, and taught him knowledge, and showed him the way of understanding?" (Isa. 40:14). When we kneel to pray and ask God to do something, he has already determined either to do that very thing or to not do it. His omniscience precludes him from learning a single thing from our prayers. Erwin Lutzer once said, "Has it ever occurred to you that nothing ever occurs to God?"[7] So here is the mystery: How does prayer change things? Basically, the only way we can understand this is that God's sovereign plan includes not only the ends but also the means to the ends. And Scripture-based, Spirit-led, passionate, prevailing prayer by an ever-increasing number of church members is God's ordained means for the revitalization of a church.

Prayer for Wisdom and Power

Two great practical concerns must always be before the hearts of God's people as they pray for church revitalization: wisdom and power.

First, we must ask for wisdom in the often tortuous road of church revitalization. James writes, "If any of you lacks wisdom, let him ask God, who gives generously to all without reproach, and it will be given him" (James 1:5). Tell God you do not know what to do to revitalize this church. It is true, isn't it? Solomon said, "I am but a little child. I do not know how to go out or come in. . . . Give your servant therefore an understanding mind to govern your people, that I might discern between good and evil" (1 Kings 3:7, 9). Such a prayer should be at the heart of a pastor who is coming into a new church revitalization situation.

Second, the revitalizing leader and all the godly people who assemble to pray should plead with God for power through the Holy Spirit to carry out God's wise plans. Sometimes we know exactly what God wants us to do, but fear of man overwhelms us and causes us to shrink back. Only the power of the Lord given in answer to prayer can cause us to make genuine progress toward revitalization.

Prayer Unifies the Godly

In any church needing revitalization, there is a divide between the regenerate and unregenerate church members. The latter tend to oppose the former at every turn in the road. But within a local church, it is divisive (and difficult) to try to cull out the godly members to unify them behind some practical initiative in church reform. Extraordinary prayer meetings are inherently attractive to the godly and repulsive to the nominal members, like a magnet attracting only metal off the floor and passing over all the dust and paper. If you want to begin drawing together a committed core of followers who are zealous for God's glory, there is nothing like a concert of prayer. A powerful spiritual benefit comes from such meetings, as well as an opportunity to build a coalition of laborers without whom no revitalization could ever occur.

PRACTICAL ADVICE

1. Use a prayer guide for revitalization, such as *Forty Days of Prayer: Devotional Guide for Church Revitalization.*[8]

2. All prayer for revitalization should begin with you: your heart, your sins, your motives, your zeal for God's glory, your knowledge of God's Word, the works God wants you to do.

3. If you are a pastor/elder called on to lead the church in revitalization, ask God to do a mighty work in your heart that leads you to a greater dependence on prayer than ever before. Repent of all prayerlessness. Ask people to pray for you.

4. If you are a layman/woman not called to up-front leadership, be faithful in praying for those who are.

5. Make the glory of God central in all your prayers for church revitalization.

6. Begin small in gathering people to pray. Gather together like-minded, committed members weekly in groups of three to five to pray for the transformation of the church. At these meetings, spend most of your time praying. You can use this time to cast a vision for the specific directions the church should go (more on that in the next chapter), but focus primarily on prayer.

7. Pray for hard-hearted opposers to be softened and transformed, or removed from the church. A key passage for this kind of prayer is 2 Timothy 2:25 (more on this in chapter 9). Since God alone has power to grant someone repentance and enable them to come to their senses and escape Satan's trap, this is a good matter for prayer.

8. Pray in light of Satan's schemes and spiritual warfare based on Ephesians 6:18. Prayer is a powerful "walkie-talkie" for spiritual warfare[9] and is one of the primary weapons God has given the church to fight the clever plans of the Evil One.

9. Believe that God can do awesome things in response to prayer. Expect him to pour out his Holy Spirit on you. Keep seeking that outpouring, as in Romans 5:5.

10. Pray personally through the directory of all church members as a daily habit. Pray for God to help you connect with people in friendship so you can persuade some to grow in their walk with Christ and be a vibrant part of the church revitalization.

8

Cast a Clear Vision

The human eye is one of the most astounding things God ever created. It is enormously complex, consisting of more than two hundred million working parts. It can process over thirty-six thousand pieces of information per hour and see perhaps as many as ten million different colors. In an average lifetime, our eyes will see twenty-four million different images. Research has found that approximately half of our brain is dedicated to processing the images our eyesight relays to it, and up to 80 percent of what we perceive about the surrounding world comes to us by our eyesight.[1] But visible light is not the only kind of light there is, just as the physical universe is not the totality of God's creation. There is an invisible, spiritual world which must also be perceived by God's servants, and the more clearly we can perceive that world, the more we will be able to live lives that glorify God. Just as the eye is the organ God created for physical vision, so faith is the organ God created for spiritual vision. Faith is the eyesight of the soul.[2]

The connection between faith and eyesight is easy to make in Scripture. Paul directly compares faith to eyesight in 2 Corinthians 5:7 when he writes, "We walk by faith, not by sight." So also in Ephesians 1:18–19, Paul prays that the "eyes of your hearts [are] enlightened," and what is this but a strengthening of our faith? Hebrews 11 asserts that by faith we see things that are invisible: "Faith is the assurance of things hoped for, the conviction of things *not seen*" (Heb. 11:1; emphasis mine). By faith, Moses "endured as *seeing* him [God] who is *invisible*" (Heb. 11:27; emphasis mine).

Spiritual vision is faith in the truths revealed in Scripture applied in specific settings. When God intends to revitalize a church, he inevitably raises up men who will step forward as visionary leaders, who by a clear vision of where God wants to bring his people are able to inspire sacrifice, suffering, and perseverance.

Why Visionary Leadership Is Vital to Revitalization

Visionary leadership is vital in all churches in order for them to bear maximum fruit for the glory of God. But it is especially essential in church revitalization situations. Such a church is overwhelmed. It has a track record of increasing weakness, a downward spiral of dwindling fruitfulness. Many of the godly members may feel powerless, aimless, and hopeless. They have lost their sense of mission and, what is far worse, their sense of God's greatness. Perhaps some unregenerate members have won the day in defining what the church is and does, leading to that downward spiral. Though visionary leadership would be essential even if that church were flourishing, never has there been so great a need for leaders to step forward and cast a biblical vision for what God is calling them to become and how he is commanding them to obey.

What Visionary Leadership Is Not

The visionary leadership I have in mind here is not the same as that called for in the secular business world. Many Christian books on leadership look to the Fortune 500 companies or cite articles in *Forbes* magazine. For example, one *Forbes* article I read recently asked, "Are You a Visionary Business Leader?" It said that vision in business "requires that you clearly see where *you choose* to be in the future and formulate the necessary steps to get your organization there. . . . A focused individual who can inspire his team to reach organizational goals is a visionary business leader"[3] (emphasis mine). Note that the "vision" for this secular business leader comes from himself. By contrast, a Christian visionary leader looks *upward to God* not *inward to himself* for his visions.

Sadly, many Christian writers scour the secular world for examples and lessons of visionary leadership.[4] They cite examples of vision, like Apple's Steve Jobs, who was a "creative genius" at telling the world what devices they could not live without but which didn't yet exist.[5] On the other side of the equation, others may cite failures in vision, like Henry Ford's sluggishness in embracing the concept that people might want to buy cars that were not painted black. This resulted in a loss of market share until he saw the error of his vision.[6] Also, Kodak failed to see the significance of digital photography for the future of its industry, which resulted in the company's financial decline. Some Christian writers scoop up such stories, write a simple list of principles for visionary leadership based on them, and perhaps include a couple of proof texts from the Bible to make it all seem Christian.

This approach fails precisely because it is secular, meaning worldly, and omits God. The vision godly leaders need to convey compellingly to the church must be of an entirely different nature. God's kingdom is not built the same way worldly empires are built. Jesus said plainly, "My kingdom is not of this world" (John 18:36).

A second caution under this heading is this: godly visionary leadership is not of the "word of faith" pattern in which we are called on to "visualize" the reality we want for the future and "by faith" speak it into existence.[7] The most popular teacher of this sort at this present time is Joel Osteen, whose book *Your Best Life Now* teaches the prosperity gospel in both old and new ways. According to Osteen, everything begins with visualization:

> The first step to living at your full potential is to enlarge your vision. To live your best life now, you must start looking at life through eyes of faith, seeing yourself rising to new levels. See your business taking off. See your marriage restored. See your family prospering. See your dreams coming to pass. You must conceive it and believe it is possible if you ever hope to experience it. . . . You will produce what you're continually seeing in your mind. . . . If you develop an image of victory, success, health, abundance, joy, peace, and happiness, nothing on earth will be able to hold those things from you. . . .

You must make room for increase in your own thinking, and then God will bring those things to pass.[8]

The visionary leadership a dying church needs is nothing of this sort. This "visualization" is barely more than our thinking we are little gods and goddesses who can create the future by picturing it in our minds.

What Godly Visionary Leadership Is

As I have already argued, true vision creates nothing. That is true in the physical world—our eyes do not create light but (if they are healthy) merely receive available light and transmit what they receive to the brain for processing. So by *vision*, I mean seeing what is true, godly, real, and ultimately, biblical. A godly visionary leader relies on Scripture and by faith sees the timeless truths of God and of his plans and purposes for all Christians generally. Along with this, the revitalizing leader is able to apply the timeless scriptural vision of God and his purposes in the world to a specific local church and its calling in that community. He is able—by the power of the Spirit of Christ in him—to say (as in Rev. 2–3), "I know your strengths and your weaknesses. I know your opportunities, what 'open door' God has set before you. I know what kind of satanic opposition assaults you. I know what kinds of secret sins are defiling you. I know you."

So this vision is of God's timeless nature and purposes, as well as the specific situation in which a given local church finds itself. What major themes are part of that vision?

The power and holiness of God. The visionary leader is able to keep clearly in front of the people, week after week from the pulpit, a clear vision of God on his throne, as Isaiah did. He is able to greatly expand their estimation of the awesome power of God enthroned, above the circle of the earth, before whom all nations are like a drop from the bucket and dust on the scales (Isa. 40:15). He is able to preach so powerfully of the holiness of God that people's consciences are searched and their lives purified by the vision. He is able to assert that God's plan and power cannot be thwarted by any created being: his plan extends over every nation on Earth and every era of human history, and his hand is stretched out with omnipotence to bring it about (Isa. 14:26–27). This is the most important vision a godly leader can impart.

The redemptive plan of God. The visionary leader is able to teach God's redemptive plan as clearly revealed in Scripture. He is able to trace out what God has done in history— from creation, through the fall and the call of Abraham and the history of the Jewish nation, to the saving work of Jesus Christ at the cross and empty tomb, to the spread of the gospel from Jerusalem to the ends of the earth (Matt. 24:14).

The nature of a healthy church. The visionary leader is able to teach what the Bible says the church should be in every generation: what it exists for, how its leadership should be characterized, what it is to do week after week, how it is to deal with sin, how it must proclaim the gospel, and how it must assemble for corporate worship, prayer, and the ministry of the Word.

The future glory of heaven. The visionary leader is able to set before the people regularly the absolute certainty of the elect being finally rescued from sin and brought into the eternal glory of the new heaven and the new earth. He is able to lay before them a vision from the book of Revelation of a perfect world and a perfect city, the New Jerusalem, so convincingly that they are able to set their minds not on earthly things but on things above and things to come (Col. 3:1–4).

Beyond these timeless themes are also two specific ones that the visionary leader must see and apply to a church needing revitalization:

Specific sins threatening the church. The visionary leader must accurately assess the specific satanic threats, sins, and weaknesses of the church. This extends to the past—the history of the church that led to it being in a weakened state and in great need of revitalization. But it includes the present and the future as well. The visionary leader must be able to read the "signs of the times" and see how Satan is sharpening specific flaming arrows of temptation through technology or current events or Supreme Court rulings or political elections or popular movements. He must also be able to see how the church may be threatened in years to come and prepare them for the inevitable attacks from the world, the flesh, and the devil.

Specific opportunities of ministry open before the church. Jesus said to the church at Philadelphia, "Behold, I have set before you an open door, which no one is able to shut" (Rev. 3:8). This represents an opportunity specific to that local church, lined up with that church's field of ministry and particular corporate gifts. A visionary leader will be able to understand the nature of the actual community where the church lives and how that church can reach out most effectively to win the lost right there. He will be filled with a buoyant hope based on the power of God that, if the church can become vibrantly healthy, it will perform the good works God has prepared in advance for them (Eph. 2:10).

Visionary Leadership Inspires Hope-Filled Sacrifice

This kind of visionary leadership is, humanly speaking, the very force that God uses to move people from fear and self-ishness to hope-filled sacrifice. It is how God has worked through leaders all throughout redemptive history. David was a visionary leader for the dispirited army of Israel when he saw clearly the zeal of God to vindicate his glory in light of the Philistine Goliath's blasphemy: "This uncircumcised Philistine shall be like one of them, for he has defied the armies of the living God" (1 Sam. 17:36). His visionary leadership moved a cowardly army to vigorous action. Nehemiah had a vision of a flourishing, rebuilt Jerusalem and was able to motivate the Jews living there to rise up, shake off fear and lethargy, and work incredibly hard to rebuild the city wall. In a like manner, Paul's courageous suffering in chains for the gospel gave courage and boldness to the brothers in the Lord to evangelize more vigorously than ever before, having lost their fear of reprisals for preaching Christ (Phil. 1:14).

The same can be said about a church needing revitalization. If the Lord is pleased with them, he will use visionary leaders to help them throw off the sin, weakness, false doctrine, and unbelief that has plagued them and follow such leaders into a new era of health and fruitfulness. No church will ever be revitalized without such leadership. And given that the way of revitalization will entail suffering and sacrifice, it is vital for the church members to see leaders who, like Paul, are willing to pay the same price in their own lives that they are calling on church members to pay. Visionary leaders must lead from the front, following their Lord, who laid down his life for the sheep.

PRACTICAL ADVICE

1. Ask God to make you a visionary leader of your local church. Ask him to show you in Scripture his own awesome power, holiness, and perfect plan. Ask him to give you a zeal for his glory that will enable you to lead others.

2. If you are a preacher, seek to convey a biblical vision for the future of the church in a wise and loving way. Do not "blow people away" before they are ready to handle it, but steadily and consistently unveil the greatness of God's purposes for your church. Make sure you root everything you say in Scripture.

3. Embrace that the people of God must have visionary leadership. Without it, the church can never make progress. God works through men who have stood in his presence and who understand his purposes.

4. If you are not a pastor, pray for God to raise up this kind of leadership in your local church. If God has already raised up a leader (or a number of leaders), support them vigorously and openly. In that way, you will be a follower-leader yourself, for others will see your example and do the same.

5. Reject worldly patterns of visionary leadership and the false "word of faith" approach of "visualization."

6. Ask God to make plain to you the specific good works that he has prepared beforehand for your church (Eph. 2:10). Seek courage and boldness to reach out in new ways to the lost in your community. As you do, ask him to open your eyes to regular patterns of outreach that the church could be doing fruitfully for years to come.

7. Understand that vision for the future comes in two categories: first, those things that most certainly will happen, because they are promised by God (e.g., all the elect will be raised up on the last day, see John 6:39); second, those things that *may* happen, because they are consistent with God's revealed will but are not guaranteed (e.g., the revitalization of your church). Emphasize the first to bring about the second.

8. As you cast a clear vision, be certain that you are leading courageously in the way you proclaim. Do not be like the scribes and Pharisees, who laid heavy burdens on others but did not lift a finger to help them (Matt. 23:4).

9

Be Humble
toward Opponents

From elementary school (when I had my last schoolyard "fight," which I lost!) until I became senior pastor of FBC, I had no human enemies. Yet, within eighteen months of beginning my ministry at this church, I had dozens of people who at least wanted me fired, perhaps sued, and it seems, possibly (based on facial expressions) dead. That experience was shocking to me. My ministry and convictions had made me many enemies.

I think it is unlikely for a work of church revitalization to go on without overcoming significant human opposition. But God commands us to be humble toward our opponents, entrusting ourselves to him. This is among the greatest displays of grace. And it will be instrumental in transforming your church.

We Wrestle Not with Flesh and Blood

Ephesians 6:10–18 is the most vital passage in the Bible on the issue of spiritual warfare. We have already asserted that the greatest threat to Satan's dark kingdom is a healthy, Bible-believing, Christ-exalting, Spirit-empowered local church. A dead church is no threat to him. Therefore, Satan will be highly motivated to fight every effort that godly leaders make in church revitalization. Welcome to the front lines of a war that's been going on for centuries!

Paul commanded the Ephesians to fight Satan by "being strong in the Lord and in the strength of his might" and by putting "on the whole armor of God" (Eph. 6:10–11). He goes on to describe this armor in great detail in verses 14–17: the belt of truth, the breastplate of righteousness, the footwear of the gospel of peace, the shield of faith, and the sword of the Spirit (the Word of God). Before describing all this weaponry, Paul makes a vital assertion for everyone involved in church revitalization to keep in mind: "We do not wrestle against flesh and blood, but against the rulers, against the authorities, against the cosmic powers over this present darkness, against the spiritual forces of evil in the heavenly places" (Eph. 6:12).

Paul was seeking to heighten the intense awareness of the Ephesian Christians to the power of our true adversary. As Martin Luther puts it so memorably in his 1529 hymn, "A Mighty Fortress Is Our God":

> For still our ancient foe doth seek to work us woe.
> His craft and power are great,
> and armed with cruel hate,
> on earth is not his equal.

> Did we in our own strength confide,
> our striving would be losing . . .

Satan is the most powerful created being, a foe powerful enough to be ruling the whole world and all of its empires by his subtle skills. The apostle John writes, "The whole world lies in the power of the evil one" (1 John 5:19). Satan's power, and the power of all his demons—"spiritual forces of evil in the heavenly realms"—is vastly greater than anything we could possibly muster or even imagine. All church revitalization is done in the face of such settled opposition in the spiritual realms.

However, when Paul writes, "We wrestle not against flesh and blood," he is making an important assertion about how we approach ministry at the human level. No one knew better than Paul how an apparent enemy of the gospel can be radically transformed to be a potent ally in a single moment by the sovereign grace of almighty God. We wage war, but our true enemies are not human beings, despite how much they may appear to be. We are at war against invisible chains of lies that Satan has used to captivate our souls (2 Cor. 10:3–5). As Keith Getty and Stuart Townend put it in their hymn, "O Church Arise," it is "our call to war, to love the captive soul," using "the sword that makes the wounded whole."[1] The captor is Satan, and his captives are people. We yearn to wield "the sword of the Spirit, which is the word of God" (Eph. 6:17) so that it makes the wounded whole.

It is easy when attacked by human beings to become angry and to pridefully fight to defend yourself, to raise your voice, to wish harm on your attacker in your heart, to delight when they fall. We can understand James and John who, when insulted by a Samaritan village that refused to welcome them, asked Jesus, "Lord, do you want us to tell fire to come down from heaven and consume them?" But Jesus rebuked them, and they simply went on to another village (Luke 9:53–54).

In the reform of FBC, I was insulted and attacked many times, and within my heart, I often felt a desire for revenge. In public settings, God gave me a special grace to respond with mildness again and again, and that greatly helped me build loyalty among others who witnessed these instances. Yet my heart was often a battlefield with fleshly desires for the total defeat of my enemies. For me, the strongest temptations were to gossip and slander in private with friends. It is so easy to tell the stories of angry attacks in such a way that the storyteller looks pure and the opponents appear purely evil. It is not hard to gather around you friends who will sympathize. But even if those allies live in another state and have no knowledge of the people you are slandering, your own heart is growing bitter with every retelling of the story. Our struggle is not against flesh and blood. We desire to see *all* the church members liberated from false doctrines and practices and brought into the glorious freedom of a truly healthy church.

Satan's Puppets in a Local Church

But that is not to say that Satan does not have his secret agents in a local church. Jesus made it clear that his enemies among the Jews were actually children of the devil who were seeking to carry out the devil's desire to kill him (John 8:44). Paul called Elymas the Sorcerer a "son of the devil" and an "enemy of all righteousness" (Acts 13:10) and struck him with blindness for his efforts at hindering the Roman proconsul, Sergius Paulus, from receiving the gospel. Jesus spoke of weeds sown among the wheat and called them "sons of the evil one, and the enemy who sowed them is the devil" (Matt. 13:38–39). Jesus said, speaking of the Pharisees, "Every plant that my heavenly Father has not planted will be rooted up" (Matt. 15:13). Satan does have his plants in every church revitalization situation. They show themselves by stubborn resistance to the truth of the Scripture and by their carnal lives. None of the bitter opponents I faced in my experience at FBC ever changed their mind and became supportive. Some who held out in neutrality were won over eventually, but no public enemies ever repented and came around. The peace-loving concepts I am presenting in this chapter are in no way seeking to minimize the damage Satan's plants can have in church revitalization.

Key Passage: 2 Timothy 2:22–26

When it came to dealing with enemies in church revitalization, no passage of Scripture was more helpful than 2 Timothy 2:22–26:

> Flee youthful passions and pursue righteousness, faith, love and peace, along with those who call on the Lord from a pure heart. Have nothing to do with foolish, ignorant controversies; you know that they breed quarrels. And the Lord's servant must not be quarrelsome but kind to everyone, able to teach, patiently enduring evil, correcting his opponents with gentleness. God may perhaps grant them repentance

leading to a knowledge of the truth, and they may come to their senses and escape from the snare of the devil, after being captured by him to do his will.

Since I was young (as many revitalizing pastors are), I needed to be told that the tendency to be prideful and hostile toward my enemies was actually an "evil desire of youth." Instead of this hostile pride, the Lord was commanding me to pursue growth in my own character—righteousness, faith, love, and peace. These qualities are in direct opposition to the carnal warlike tendencies of vengeance, factionalism, gossip, slander, underhanded tactics, and contentiousness. God wanted me to keep my heart pure by calling on his name. And he was commanding me to shun "foolish, ignorant controversies" that produce quarrels. How easy it is to quarrel during a church revitalization—to argue this text of Scripture versus that or to make your point as in a boxing match. But "the Lord's servant must not be quarrelsome." How often I was restrained by that one verse! Instead, God told me to be "kind to everyone, able to teach, not resentful." These three commands will serve every church leader well until the end of time. Show kindness, not harshness and vindictiveness. The ability to make a clear argument from Scripture is essential in demolishing false ideas and healing the people who are holding them. All the while, you must shun resentfulness. How that command reached my heart to its core! It was incredibly easy to feel resentful about the unfair attacks I was receiving as a servant of the Lord!

The final section of 2 Timothy 2:22–26 spoke most eloquently of all—we must correct with gentleness those who oppose us as church leaders. This directly connects with the "able to teach" that Paul writes about earlier in the passage. We must not play the nice-guy role as though their liking us personally is the goal. We must not shrink back from teaching clearly the Scriptures, which alone have the power to transform that church; instead, we must instruct "with gentleness," with a tenderness and meekness that will be maximally attractive to those who have never heard these things before.

And we do so in the hope that the Word of God will liberate people from Satan's secret bondage. We yearn for their heartfelt repentance, which is something only God can give. That is why church revitalization can be done only by the sovereign power of God over a human heart. That "God may perhaps grant them repentance" is the deepest longing of our hearts as we face human opposition. We believe those who oppose us must come to their senses, for all sin is a form of spiritual insanity. Clarity of mind comes only by the ministry of the Word and the Holy Spirit. And if God should give such clarity, these people who were formerly taken captive by the devil to do the will of God will be, at last, liberated to serve him!

Love Your Enemies

Many passages in Scripture command us to love our enemies. Jesus directly said this in Matthew 5:44: "Love your enemies and pray for those who persecute you." In so doing we will imitate our heavenly Father and grow toward the perfection that salvation in Christ will eventually complete in us (Matt. 5:48). So also Paul forbids the taking of revenge and commands us richly to do good to those who hate us (Rom.

12:19–20). The final word in that paragraph is amazingly helpful in bitter church settings: "Do not be overcome by evil, but overcome evil with good" (Rom. 12:21). Only good can drive out evil, just as only light can drive out darkness. If when we are attacked we respond in kind, we are no different than they are. All that has happened is that evil has become even more deeply entrenched in that church.

Why Be Humble toward Opponents? Ten Good Reasons.

(1) *Because God opposes the proud but gives grace to the humble* (1 Pet. 5:5). God detests pride in any form, and if church revitalizers are more zealous for their own agenda than God's glory, God will fight them as much as he will fight the nominal Christians at that church. But God gives grace to the humble. So humble yourself, and God will lift you up.

(2) *Because we are sinners too.* Every church leader, no matter how godly, is a sinner saved by grace. We all deserve eternal condemnation. How are we different from those who oppose us? Is there any sin that we see in our opponents that we are incapable of? "Who sees anything different in you? What do you have that you did not receive? If then you received it, why do you boast as if you did not receive it?" (1 Cor. 4:7). Meditation on God's grace in your own life should destroy any arrogance you may feel toward your opponents.

(3) *Because God is motivated to fight for those who do not fight for themselves.* In this way, we will be following the example of Jesus Christ and how he treated his enemies. According to 1 Peter 2:23, "When he was reviled, he did not revile in return; when he suffered, he did not threaten, but

continued entrusting himself to him who judges justly." In entrusting ourselves to him who judges justly, we are forsaking the right to defend ourselves. God's wisdom and power in defending those falsely attacked when serving him are beyond our calculation. And God will use our humble suffering to advance his purposes in the church.

(4) *Because Paul was willing to trade his salvation to rescue his enemies.* In Romans 9:1–4, the apostle Paul made a stunning claim—that, if possible, he was willing to trade his own salvation and spend eternity in hell if it would result in the salvation of his Jewish enemies. He claimed to have "great sorrow and unceasing anguish" in his heart concerning their spiritual condition. Paul is a great role model for any leader in church revitalization. Paul's Jewish enemies were hunting him down to kill him. Ours are doing far less. We should see our opponents in light of eternity—and yearn to win them over to Christ.

(5) *You cannot tell the wheat from the weeds.* In Christ's parable about the wheat and the weeds, the mixed nature of the world—sons of God and sons of the devil—could not be remedied before the end of the age. The servants offered to pull up the weeds; the master said, "No, lest in gathering the weeds you root up the wheat along with them" (Matt. 13:29). This clearly indicates that before the end of the age, we will not be able to tell the difference between wheat and weeds. Paul, the greatest servant of Christ that has ever lived, was initially the most vicious persecutor of Christians on Earth. God's grace can win anyone at any time. Today's hate-filled enemy may be tomorrow's zealous co-laborer. And it is "speaking the truth in love" (Eph. 4:15) that God will use to win them.

(6) *You are not the issue; God's glory is.* When we pride-fully rise up to defend our honor, we are acting as though that is more important than the glory of God in the revitalization of a church for whom Christ shed his blood.

(7) *A humble response to attacks will motivate church members to join you.* If you respond to mean-spirited at-tacks in a like manner, it will be obvious to everyone that you are no different than your enemies. But if you are filled with the Spirit, speaking only scriptural truths, and seek-ing repentance and reconciliation with every person, quiet observers will be strongly motivated to come to your aid in the church revitalization process.

(8) *Your enemies may be right . . . about something.* It is exceptionally humble to listen to your adversaries with the conviction that they have something worth listening to. While we may disagree about the most fundamental issues having to do with the gospel or the scriptural principles of healthy church life, they may have a valid perspective that God wants you to heed regarding some key aspect of the issues or of your own demeanor or performance. God can speak anytime through anyone. For example, God enabled wicked Caiaphas to prophesy accurately about Christ (John 11:49–52). If God can speak through someone like Caiaphas, he can speak to a church leader in the midst of difficult church revitalization work.

George Whitefield was one of the most attacked ministers of the gospel in history. Everywhere he went, enemies rose up to oppose the new work God was doing through Whitefield in his preaching the new birth to thousands of people outside church buildings. Yet whenever enemies would bring some bitter charge against him, instead of dismissing it out of hand, saying, "I am doing a great work for God," he would take in carefully whatever they would say and humbly promise to pray over their accusations. He would then in private spread those assaults before God in prayer and would in effect say, "Search me, O God, and know my heart! Try me and know my thoughts!" (Ps. 139:23–24). He would listen to the Spirit most humbly, as the Spirit separated the wheat from the chaff in the accusation. He would then repent based on the genuine critiques and disregard the rest.

If some enemy comes to you after a particularly challenging meeting and says you were rude or you misrepresented their position or you did not follow *Robert's Rules of Order*[2] or you did something else they don't approve of, be humble, take their input, and repent when you must.

(9) *Humility will adorn the gospel for outsiders to see.* We never know who is watching us as we carry on our work of revitalization. And the world is watching the church all the time to see if we practice what we preach. Titus 2:10 says that Christians can "adorn the doctrine of God our Savior" by how we act. If you are genuinely humble in dealing with in-church opposition, the Lord will make it obvious to the community at some point and use you to bring some lost person to Christ.

(10) *Suffering well grows you in Christlikeness.* Never forget that the ministry God gives us is as much a part of our own salvation process as it is a part of the salvation of others. We are not done being sanctified, and God uses these kinds of bitter trials to conform us to the likeness of his Son, Jesus Christ. That is why Romans 5:3 says that "suffering produces endurance." We need to be thankful for our enemies because God is using them to shape our souls for his glory.

Fight for the Truth

God does not will for us to give in for an instant on issues of biblical truth. It is not humility but self-serving coward-ice that causes us to back down from doctrinal attacks. We must fight like lions for the truth of the gospel—the souls of our hearers are at stake. Paul is a prime example of this in Galatians 1–2, as he fought not only the Judaizers and their false "gospel" of works but also had to oppose publicly Peter and Barnabas and some good brothers within the church who were being led astray (Gal. 2:11–13). Paul writes, "We did not yield in submission even for a moment, so that the truth of the gospel might be preserved for you" (Gal. 2:5). Where biblical truth is at stake, we must fight with great perseverance. I have been advocating humility on issues of personal conduct. But when it comes to doctrine, we must follow Luther's example: "Unless I am convinced by scripture and plain reason . . . my conscience is captive to the Word of God. I cannot and I will not recant anything for to go against conscience is neither right nor safe. God help me. Amen."[3]

PRACTICAL ADVICE

1. Make it a point to obey Jesus's command to pray for those who oppose and insult you. Pray for them by name. Pray for God to grant them repentance and the knowl-edge of the truth (2 Tim. 2:25–26). Read over Romans 9:1–4, and ask God to work in your heart the same level of self-denying grief that Paul had over the spiritual state of his lost opponents.

2. Follow George Whitefield's practice of bringing all criticisms back to God in prayer. Pray Psalm 139:23–24 over each one. Where you are convicted that you have wronged someone, be humble enough to go back to that person and seek forgiveness.

3. Practice good listening skills with people who disagree with you. Repeat back to them what you think they are saying to be sure you are getting it right.

4. Ask the Lord in prayer to give you a discerning heart to know when to fight like a lion (over biblical doctrine) and when to be humble and yielding. Even when you do feel the need to fight like a lion, do so with "gentleness and respect" (1 Pet. 3:15) toward your opponents. You are seeking to demolish false ideas, not people.

5. Get prepared for potentially contentious meetings, especially before the whole church (like in church conferences), by praying in great detail about what you're about to face, putting on the spiritual armor Paul lists in Ephesians 6:10–17, and by reading many Scripture verses on humility.

6. Be especially wary of gossip and slander when gathered with passionate supporters of your efforts at church revitalization. Understand how sinful it is to act as though you could never commit the same sins that they do.

7. Ponder the example of the Pharisee and the tax collector in Jesus's parable of humble prayer (Luke 18:9–14). One trusted in his own righteousness and said, "I thank you that I am not like other men," while the other refused to look up to heaven, but beat his breast and said, "Be

merciful to me, a sinner." Which of the two are you most like when it comes to your opponents?

8. Understand that some opponents really are children of the devil and will never be reconciled to biblical doctrine. But also know that some of the bitterest enemies right now could become staunch allies later.

9. Read Paul's prohibition passage in 1 Corinthians 6:1–8 and submit to God's wisdom. Meditate often on Paul's statement, "Why not rather be wronged?" It will carry you a long way in dealing well with your enemies.

10. As you proceed in church revitalization, be more and more zealous for Christ's glory than for your good reputation among others.

10

Be Courageous

I am inspired by great stories of courage. I remember reading once of the stunning courage of Alexander the Great in a battle he fought in India. Angry at the reticence of his weary men to take a walled Multanese citadel in eastern Punjab, Alexander himself vaulted over the wall and into the compound where he faced the enraged enemy soldiers alone for a few shocking moments. Ashamed of their weakness in the face of their king's courage, Alexander's soldiers stormed in after him and rescued him, winning the battle. Alexander himself was badly wounded and seemed close to death. Nonetheless, he survived, and the loyalty among his soldiers was never greater. Such accounts of battlefield courage fill the pages of military history.

I believe the greatest stories in history are connected with the advance of the gospel of Jesus Christ. Part of the joy of heaven will be to recount the great exploits of the saints for the glory of God and to celebrate the courage they have shown in advancing the kingdom of God: "They loved not their lives even unto death" (Rev. 12:11).

If you are called by God to be involved in the great work of church revitalization, you are called to a life of courage. No dying church will ever be revitalized without courage, for Satan never gives up any territory without a fight. If you want to be part of what God is doing to reclaim that lost territory, you must be willing to face attacks of the devil with great courage—a boldness that only God can give.

John Bunyan's *Pilgrim's Progress* includes a character named Mr. Valiant-for-Truth. This incredible warrior for the truth of the gospel represents clearly the courage that all faithful servants of the Lord must have in fighting the Lord's battles. In what is effectively his "Last Will and Testament," Mr. Valiant-for-Truth bequeaths his "sword" to those who would follow: that is, the Word of God. Then he offers his courage and skill to whoever could obtain it. This is a timeless challenge to all of us who follow the heroes of the faith to rise up and carry on the noble reconquest of the world from Satan's clutches. No one can achieve anything for the Lord without that courage and skill. Then Mr. Valiant-for-Truth says these unforgettable words: "My Marks and Scars I carry with me, to be a witness for me that I have fought his Battles who now will be my Rewarder."[1]

None of the valiant brothers and sisters who have suffered and died for Christ in generations past can bequeath us their wounds. Now is our time; this is our battle. And the wounds we will receive in life and ministry will be a witness for us that we have fought battles for the same Lord they served.

Overcoming Fear of Man

Now, realistically, what kinds of trials face us? What must we overcome? Predominantly, the attack will come through fear of man. Satan uses human beings in an intimidating way, and the fear of man is a powerful hindrance to the work of church reform. At every step, we are tempted to wonder, *What will so and so think? What will the deacons do? Will people leave the church if I preach such and such?* I certainly asked those questions. The leader of the faction that opposed me was a man with a powerful temper, who more than once displayed visible rage at me. Once, when we were riding in a car together and I tried to broach the subject of the growing controversy at church, his driving became erratic, and he yelled at me, "I will fight you every step of the way." This was no idle boast. He used to sit with his arms crossed and glare at me while I preached. At one point, however, I realized that he would never be pleased with me no matter what I preached; his real problem was with the Lord—not with me.

Scripture clearly testifies to the danger of fear of man: Paul said, "Am I now seeking the approval of man, or of God? Or am I trying to please man? If I were still trying to please man, I would not be a servant of Christ" (Gal. 1:10). The Lord made it clear to me that I needed to learn to fear him more than I feared any man. To shrink back from a great work of church reform because I was afraid of what would happen to me was shameful. To hesitate to preach any truth of the Bible because of fear of man was to contribute to the church's slide toward spiritual oblivion. God used a clear passage in Isaiah to warn me that I needed to fear him more than any man who could oppose me: "I, I am he who comforts you;

who are you that you are afraid of man who dies, of the son of man who is made like grass, and have forgotten the LORD, your Maker, who stretched out the heavens and laid the foundations of the earth" (Isa. 51:12–13).

Suffering and Eternal Rewards

One of the greatest inducements to embracing suffering with courage is the doctrine of the eternal rewards that God promises to all who suffer for Christ. Christ desires very much that we set our hearts on the rewards he will give all who serve him faithfully on Earth. If he did not want us to yearn for those rewards, why would he tell us so much of them? The more courageously we suffer for Christ on Earth, the greater will be our reward in heaven: "Blessed are you when others revile you and persecute you and utter all kinds of evil against you falsely on my account. Rejoice and be glad, for your reward is great in heaven, for so they persecuted the prophets who were before you" (Matt. 5:11–12). It is interesting to me that the Lord mentions such things as insults and people falsely saying evil things against us. Those are just words, yet bearing patiently under them results in a great reward in heaven. It is highly unlikely for anyone to engage in church revitalization without facing slander, false accusations, insults, and verbal attacks. God will reward all who endure them courageously.

Courage Displayed in Heroes from the Bible

Contemplating the faith-filled heroes of the Bible gives us examples to follow; it feeds our faith and motivates us to follow their example. This is the clear purpose of the author of Hebrews 11 and his great "Hall of Faith." He cites one example after another of men and women who lived and died by faith. It took great courage for Abram to leave Ur of the Chaldees and go to an unknown land. And it took even more courage for him to sacrifice his miracle son, Isaac, as obedience to the command of God. Moses showed courage in repeatedly facing Pharaoh with the bold command, "Thus says the LORD, the God of Israel, 'Let my people go!'" (Ex. 5:1). And it took even more courage for him to lead Israel through the Red Sea in the dark of night, with the sea walled up to their left and right. Joshua displayed courage in the battles that followed Israel's crossing of the Jordan River. David's example of facing Goliath with a sling and five smooth stones motivated a cowardly army to rise up and defeat the Philistines. The prophets showed courage repeatedly in confronting the wicked kings of Israel and Judah. Perhaps no one in the Old Testament was called to greater suffering for the Word than Jeremiah, who stood courageously again and again to preach to a hard-hearted nation that God had already told him would never believe him. Shadrach, Meshach, and Abednego stood courageously against the tyrant king Nebuchadnezzar and were willing to die rather than disobey God.

So also the New Testament is filled with stories of great courage. We can point to the boldness of John the Baptist in confronting Herod in his sin or the amazing advance of the gospel in the book of Acts by the boldness of the apostles or the courage shown by the apostle Paul in facing death multiple times for preaching Christ.

Of course, no one in all of human history has shown as much courage as Jesus Christ did in Gethsemane and at the cross. What happened at Gethsemane? Jesus had known all his life that he would die on the cross. But the full revelation of what that would be like was withheld from him until Gethsemane. I believe that when Jesus began to pray, God revealed to him in an immeasurably vivid way what it would be like to die on the cross as a substitute for his sheep, drinking the cup of God's wrath poured full strength for him, and it shocked him.[2] It was akin to the difference between reading a verbal description of the Grand Canyon and seeing an IMAX movie of a helicopter ride through the Grand Canyon. This intense revelation literally knocked Jesus to the ground and so increased the stress in his body that blood began to flow from his sweat pores and fell in great drops to the ground (Luke 22:44). The Father did this, I believe, to give Christ the ability to make a more informed choice as to whether he would go through with their plan. God refrained from fully revealing it sooner because the level of mental anguish would have been too great for Jesus's human nature to bear for any great length of time.

Let's also remember one of the most heroic moments in human history: when Jesus prayed, "My Father, if it be possible, let this cup pass from me; nevertheless, not as I will, but as you will" (Matt. 26:39). At this moment, Christ put his own will completely under the will of his Father; he then rose and went to the cross to drink the cup of God's infinite wrath.[3] Though anything we do in service to Christ will be infinitely less courageous than this, we are called on to take up our own crosses and die to our own comforts and pleasures as he did. Without such a commitment, no church revitalization will ever happen.

Inspiration from the Heroes of Church History

To some degree, there is a level of shame in writing about the "courage" involved in revitalizing a church in some comfortable community in our prosperous country. The worst that can happen to us here is a lot of hostility, anger, perhaps a lawsuit, and eviction from a ministry or from membership in that church. Physical attacks are highly unlikely, as is actual death.

But we belong to a royal lineage of brothers and sisters who have gone before us and have suffered almost indescribable pain to advance the kingdom of Christ. During my days of trial at FBC, I drew a great measure of inspiration from the heroes of church history. I read often about the martyrs who died during the Roman persecution, of whom Tertullian said, "The blood of martyrs is seed."[4] I read of Polycarp, who courageously faced being burned at the stake with the words, "Eighty-six years have I been serving him, and he has done me no wrong; how then can I blaspheme my king who saved me?"[5] After I read those words the day of one of our bitter and heart-wrenching church conferences, I felt a surge of courage and a desire not to act shamefully in my time of trial, however insignificant it was compared to Jesus's. I read missionary biographies and suffered along with Adoniram Judson, who was shackled by iron chains for eleven months in the death prison of Ava in Burma for preaching the gospel, tormented constantly by stench and biting insects, sometimes hung upside down by his feet.[6] In light of such stories, it is hard to feel sorry for yourself because a few unregenerate church members have falsely accused you or yelled at you in the fellowship hall. I read of William Tyndale, a fugitive from the king of England for the "crime" of translating the Bible into English, who was betrayed, arrested, imprisoned through a fierce winter, and at last burned at the stake. As he was dying in torment, he prayed most powerfully and lovingly, "Lord, open the King of England's eyes!"[7] How could I behave with less dignity amid the vastly inferior trial of church revitalization in America?

We are surrounded by "so great a cloud of witnesses" (Heb. 12:1), whose record of faith and courage glorifies the same Lord I yearn to serve. I want to live as courageously for him as they did.

PRACTICAL ADVICE

1. Expect to suffer and face opposition in church revitalization. Therefore, expect that you will need courage.
2. Be honest to God in prayer about your lack of courage and fear of man. Ask him to grant you the courage you need to speak and act when the Spirit moves.
3. Meditate much on pleasing God until your fear of man shrinks to a manageable size.
4. Memorize Scripture that will enable you to see each situation with eyes of faith.
5. Develop an eternal perspective, and set your heart fully on the grace to be given you at the second coming of Christ (Col. 3:1–2; 1 Pet. 1:13).

6. Study Hebrews 11 and absorb the lessons of courage and faith from the faith-filled men and women celebrated in that chapter. They are the "cloud of witnesses" (Heb. 12:1) that surrounds you.

7. Worship Christ for the astonishing courage he showed in Gethsemane, when God revealed the scope and magnitude of what it would be like to drink the cup of his wrath on the cross. Ask God to open your heart to such courage by the Spirit.

8. Meditate on the rewards Christ will give, even to those who are insulted and slandered falsely for his sake (Matt. 5:11–12). Long for those rewards, which will be praise from God (1 Cor. 4:5).

9. Study heroes from church history and learn how they displayed courage. Let their examples shrink your fear and raise your zeal to live with boldness for the glory of the same Lord they served.

10. Meditate on Paul's "weakness and . . . fear and much trembling" as a display of the power of the Spirit in him to do God's will (1 Cor. 2:3).

11. Understand that courage is not the absence of fear but the ability to overcome fear to do what God has set before you. Expect to feel butterflies in your stomach.

12. Do not underestimate the value of humor! I had a co-laborer in church revitalization named Josh Smith whose father had been president of the SBC during a particularly contentious time. On one occasion, as we were getting ready to go down to our fellowship hall, I expressed my fear of facing all those hostile people. He said with a twinkle in his eye and a smile on his lips,

"Don't worry. If anyone comes after you, I'll give them the 'Atomic Elbow!'" and he showed me some wrestling move. I laughed but then said, "They're not going to attack me. They're just going to give me evil looks." He said, "I can do that too! How is this for the 'evil eye'?" and he gave me the most comical look in which one eye was bulging bigger than the other. We walked into the room laughing—and the fear was gone.

11

Be Patient

Recently, I was sitting in an airport reading a book describing the Atlantic crossing made by the *Mayflower* in 1620. It vividly detailed the heaving waves, cold, seasickness, and impossibility of the pilgrims cooking any hot meals in the dark, foul-smelling, vomit-covered area below deck where they were enduring the passage. As I was absorbed in this account, I overheard a well-dressed businessman walking by me talking loudly about the experience he had just suffered through. "It was a total nightmare!" he said. "We sat in the plane on the tarmac for almost an hour before we were finally cleared for takeoff. Now I have an extra two-hour layover as a result!" I laughed to myself as he angrily bustled by. The pilgrims in my story had a sixty-six-day voyage in the most wretched conditions, then landed on Cape Cod in November, hurriedly constructed some structures to protect them through the winter, and ended up burying 51 out of the 102 members of their community during that harsh winter of 1620–21. Their patience in suffering was astonishing. But here we struggle with an additional delay and a two-hour layover in an air-conditioned lounge in an airport. If anything, the instant gratification fed by fast food, internet browsing, electronic entertainment, smartphones, and all other manner of labor-saving devices has made us even more impatient.

No church revitalization can be effective without a great deal of patience. This is especially difficult for the young and inexperienced men God frequently calls on to lead the church through a labyrinth of complex changes. Their zeal for the changes needed might greatly outstrip their wisdom in sequencing those changes and their patience in waiting for them to come about.

God's Patience in Salvation

The God of the Bible is stunningly patient. He has worked out a meticulous plan and is unfolding it at the perfect pace, according to his own wisdom. All the aspects of this comprehensive plan were worked out to the minutest detail before God created heaven and earth (Eph. 1:11). God waited four centuries for the "iniquity of the Amorites" to reach its full measure (Gen. 15:16) before he fulfilled his promise to Abraham to bring his descendants into the Promised Land. All that time, the Jews were languishing in slavery in Egypt, crying out, "How long, O Lord?" Once they came out of Egypt, because of their sin of unbelief, God made them wait another forty years before their children could take possession of their inheritance (Num. 32:13). And their subsequent history in the Promised Land shows God's amazing forbearance in dealing with their persistent sin.

God waited for millennia until just the right moment in history for the Savior of the world, Jesus Christ, to be born of a woman (Gal. 4:4). Since that time, God has been slowly but irresistibly saving the elect from every tribe and language, people and nation. And all that time, God has "endured with much patience vessels of wrath prepared for destruction" (Rom. 9:22) who are resisting the gospel and making life miserable for his people.

The apostle Peter writes plainly about the reason for God's amazing patience: "The Lord is not slow to fulfill his promise as some count slowness, but is patient toward you, not wishing that any should perish, but that all should reach repentance" (2 Pet. 3:9). Every leader in church revitalization must learn to curb impatience with a heavenly perspective of knowing that God's purpose is to work salvation in all his elect, and there is a perfect time for each of his elect to be brought into the kingdom. Think of how God—by his sovereign grace and with a radiant display of the glory of the resurrected Christ—could have converted Saul of Tarsus at any time. But he willed that Saul persecute the church in the precise manner that he did, and for as many days as he did, to establish his reputation as an enemy of the gospel who was then converted only as a display of Christ's unlimited patience (1 Tim. 1:16).

As God's servants, we must be conformed to his patience and allow his timing to have sway. He hears all our prayers and sees all our tears; he knows how people are making life miserable for the church reformers, what slanderous attacks they are using. He will use all of their bitter attacks to shape his elect and, if he wills, to revitalize that church at just the right time.

The Fruit of the Spirit

The patience required for church renewal is supernatural, and it is biblical for us to see it as the direct work of the Holy Spirit in us. Paul asserts that the "fruit of the Spirit" includes "patience," sometimes translated "longsuffering" (Gal. 5:22). As we walk in the power of the Holy Spirit, he enables us to rest humbly and submissively under his mighty hand so that "at the proper time" (i.e., when his perfect timing comes) he may exalt us (1 Pet. 5:6). The humility required for this waiting is also supernatural, and it stems from realizing that Christ is the King and we are merely his servants. It is often necessary for all church revitalizers to wait on the Lord in prayer, pleading with him to give us his perspective—and his patience. The Lord knows how hasty and impatient we are; how arrogant it would be to think that we know best, that *right now* is the best time. When we are tempted to move ahead of God, we must realize that we will only do damage to the perfect plans he has laid out for our church: "Wait for the LORD and keep his way" (Ps. 37:34).

The Parables: Waiting for the Tender Plant to Grow

Many of our Savior's parables are agricultural—seeds planted, various types of soil used, growth displayed or not, harvest time coming at last (Matt. 13:24–31; Mark 4:3–9; Luke 13:6–9; 21:19–31; John 12:24). These liken the kingdom of heaven to the secret processes worked only by the power of God on plants to bring them to full fruition. Mark 4:26–29 is a clear example:

> The kingdom of God is as if a man should scatter seed on the ground. He sleeps and rises night and day, and the seed sprouts and grows; he knows not how. The earth produces by itself, first the blade, then the ear, then the full grain in the ear. But when the grain is ripe, at once he puts in the sickle, because the harvest has come.

This parable is amazingly helpful for all servants of God to ponder and absorb, but especially for those committed to church revitalization. The secret work of the kingdom of God is likened to a seed sown by a farmer in the ground. In this parable, once the seed is sown, the farmer's task is complete. Jesus's words systematically eliminate his will, effort, skill, and even involvement. The seed grows "night and day." The farmer is not coaxing growth out of this seed. As a matter of fact, when the seed sprouts and grows, Jesus asserts clearly that the farmer "knows not how." It grows *all by itself.*

This is extremely humbling to us who feel that our constant efforts are essential to the revitalization of a church. God *means* to humble us in the work of revitalization. The essence of the transformation from dying to vibrantly alive is a secret transformation in the hearts of most of its members by the Spirit of God. What do we know about that? How can we effect it, guarantee it, advance it, bring it about, take any credit for it at all? And as the little seed is growing from the ground, the only thing we can do is destroy it. Imagine if the farmer, trembling with eagerness, went out hour after hour to inspect his garden. Imagine his delight as he finally sees a tender, green shoot poke its fragile head through the soil. But if this man is impatient, instead of allowing God's orderly process—"first the blade, then the ear, then the full grain in the ear"—he takes hold of the tiny, moist, green tendril and begins to tug at it, saying aloud, "Come on, grow! Now!" All he will do is kill it.

So it is too with the gradual work of revitalization. Little by little, previously immature believers are gaining a glimpse of the majestic doctrines of God. They are seeing more and more clearly the stunning grace of God in Christ crucified and resurrected. They are seeing the depth of their own sin for the first time but are also assured of God's infinitely deep mercy in Christ. They are seeing their place in God's plan, and the biblical design for the church is emerging more and more clearly through the ministry of the Word of God and the indwelling Holy Spirit. Impatience will ruin the orderly progression God has in mind. In the fullness of time will come the rich harvest of spiritual maturity. Not before.

Better Patience than Strength and Courage

Many young men in their first pastorate find themselves in dysfunctional churches, with all manner of doctrinal errors and lifestyle corruptions. Their zeal for a healthy church burns within them, but so does their insecurity and desire to prove themselves faithful to their Master. They want to prove their courage and strength, along with their loyalty. They are ready to fall on a sword for Jesus. But are they ready to be patient instead, to *not* fall on the sword but to offer themselves as a "living sacrifice" (Rom. 12:1) of patience?

Most church revitalization issues call for more patience than courage and strength. Two proverbs make this point far better than I can: "Whoever is slow to anger is better than the mighty, and he who rules his spirit than he who takes a city" (Prov. 16:32), and "With patience a ruler may be persuaded, and a soft tongue will break a bone" (Prov. 25:15). Each of these shows the value of patience over courage and strength in certain settings. Young men often want to prove their valor by strong assertions, uncompromising stands, and a willingness to be fired for upholding a doctrinal principle. But it may well be that the Lord wants you to show patience, humility, and a willingness to control your temper, overlook an insult, and persuade with gentle words.

"I Still Have Many Things to Say to You"

Every godly pastor has to be eager to proclaim anything the Bible teaches and to not shrink back from proclaiming the whole counsel of God's Word (Acts 20:20, 27). But there is a difference between a coward who shrinks back out of fear and a wise shepherd who patiently allows time for the people to grow up under a steady diet of faithful biblical instruction until they are increasingly more able to hear anything God says. A plain example of this is found in Jesus's tenderness toward his disciples the night before he was crucified. He said, "I still have many things to say to you, but you cannot bear them now" (John 16:12). It is vital for all pastors to ponder this wise sense of what Jesus's beloved children can handle! It is not cowardly to wait until spiritual infants grow up from milk to meat. Jesus also plainly said that the additional doctrines he wanted to impart to them, for which they were not yet ready, he would most certainly teach them in due time through the coming Spirit (John 16:13).

Earning Trust

Practically speaking, then, a new pastor must first settle in and earn the trust of his congregation. A revitalizing pioneer challenges cherished presuppositions and seemingly shakes the very foundation of all the congregation has assumed and held dear for years. As the men of Athens put it, "You bring some strange ideas to our ears. We wish to know therefore what these things mean" (Acts 17:20). A pastor needs to know what the people of his church believe regarding some of the more controversial doctrines of the Bible and to be patient in how and when to unfold them: election, predestination, reprobation, the millennium, divorce/remarriage, gender and authority, homosexuality, abortion, church discipline, polity, etc. Wisdom calls for earning the people's trust by initially teaching the simple truths of the gospel in a verse-by-verse manner, then steadily building out from there. The pastor can mention these controversial doctrines as they arise in the text and be faithful to what the Bible teaches without elaborating in depth.

When I began my pulpit ministry at FBC, I started with a series in 2 Timothy called "Boldness and Faithfulness in the Gospel." The book is Paul's sweet and tenderhearted farewell to Timothy, his beloved son in the faith. It contains hardly any controversial doctrines, so it was a good place for me to start preaching to a new congregation. I went from there to a verse-by-verse exposition of the Gospel of Matthew. Week after week, I was earning trust by a faithful and straightforward handling of text after text. The goal is to be patient and wait for the congregation to get more and more accustomed to hearing plainly whatever God's Word says.

Luther and the Idols of the Heart

When Luther was preaching, writing, and leading the Protestant Reformation in Wittenberg, the primacy he placed on the Word of God caused people to rethink almost everything to do with their worship patterns. This included statues of saints or other objects of worship. Some overly zealous mobs, enflamed with resentment against Roman Catholic leaders, began to roam from church to church destroying all such objects of veneration. They unleashed a torrent of disorderly violence that Luther worked vigorously to stop. He preached very plainly on how the details of the reformation of public worship should be done. He said, in effect, "Take care of the idols of the heart, and the idols on the wall will take care of themselves."[1] It takes patience to allow God's Word to drive out the idols of the heart; premature so-called "courageous" actions can rupture church unity and spell the early end of a promising ministry. It is far better for the people to see what needs reforming in the church and do it themselves as led by the Word and the Spirit.

An example of this at FBC had to do with some pictures of Jesus that were hanging up in key places near our sanctuary. These showed Jesus as Caucasian, with flowing, shimmering blond hair in profile, as though he had sat for a portrait. The

Bible contains no physical descriptions of Jesus and such a painting was, in my opinion, an idol on the wall. I felt (as did others) that it could be a stumbling block to the many different nationalities and races of people who had been regularly attending worship. But if I had acted too boldly and taken matters into my own hands early in my ministry, I would have offended many. Instead, I taught on idolatry (especially in 1 John 5:21: "Little children, keep yourselves from idols") and waited for God's Word to take effect. One day, those pictures were gone. To this day, I do not know who took them down or where they were taken. I say that with a completely clear conscience. But they are gone, and I did not do it.

Two Case Studies

There are two case studies from FBC's history in which it was valuable for us to have had patience in church revitalization. The first is church discipline, and the second is a transition to a plurality of elders.

When it comes to church discipline, it should be obvious how rash it would be for a new pastor to move unilaterally in instituting reformation to a biblical standard. That churches should practice church discipline is clear from Matthew 18:15–17 and 1 Corinthians 5. That most churches needing revitalization have not practiced biblical church discipline in years (if ever) is almost as clear. If a new pastor thinks that reestablishing this practice should occur immediately in his ministry, he is taking a short route to his own eviction. First of all, if the church does not understand why we should practice biblical church discipline, in what manner, by what procedures, and with what motives, even if the church follows the pastor and does what he wants, great damage will be done. More likely, however, the church will rebel and fight him. Since church discipline is done by the whole church and not only the pastor, the congregation must be well prepared to do its vital work. So at FBC, we did not try to do any church discipline until the church had been instructed on it for years and was essentially unified.

In the second case, the transition from a single elder model to the biblical norm of plural elders at FBC came over many years of consistent teaching. From the beginning of my ministry at FBC, I made it clear that I believed in plural elders, but I did so only in private conversations and in passing references in sermons and Bible studies. I made it especially clear in my training of other leaders. The concept was extremely strange to many church members—they felt it was much more Presbyterian than Baptist. However, once the struggle concerning biblical faithfulness was won (by 2002), I began teaching and leading much more openly toward plurality of elders. I taught on church polity on Wednesday evenings and began training many godly men in this structure. I preached sermons on it on Sunday evenings, and then, when the time was right, on Sunday mornings as well. I began calling on the church to change its polity toward this model and supported it multiple times with Scripture. I was greatly aided by other godly men who understood this as the biblical norm. We met together in a group to draw up a whole new set of bylaws for the church centered on plural elders as the leadership structure. We had three different "town meetings" to discuss this change and answer any questions. We waited for several months to clear any objections anyone might have. By that third town meeting, there was total silence at the Q&A time. The congregation was simply ready—eagerly ready—to make the vote. It did so, and more than 90 percent of the congregation accepted the change. That was the fruit of patience.

Bypassing Rabaul . . . for Now

On January 23, 1942, the Imperial Japanese army captured the city of Rabaul, the capital of New Britain in the Solomon Islands of the South Pacific. Their invading force was twenty thousand strong, and they immediately fortified it with many ships and planes. As American military leaders were planning the war in the Pacific, they initially felt it absolutely imperative to recapture Rabaul. But the invasion plans drawn up by General Douglas MacArthur called for tens of thousands of troops and two aircraft carriers. As the war unfolded, it became evident how costly it would be to recapture this awesome fortress. Soon war planners in Washington, DC, came up with a stunning alternative. Why not bypass Rabaul altogether and move closer to Japan using other, more lightly defended islands as stepping-stones to final victory? Bypassing Rabaul set the stage for the "island-hopping" strategy used by Douglas MacArthur and Chester Nimitz for the rest of the war—ultimately saving thousands of lives and hastening the end of the war.

When it comes to church revitalization, sometimes it is wiser to bypass a controversial issue that really does not matter for the sake of the long-term transformation of the church. Some people in dying churches—mostly traditionalists who are clinging to a bygone era—will fight tooth and nail over minor issues. At FBC, these disagreements were in regard to such things as traditional services at the Fourth of July and Christmas (the Moravian Love Feast), the use of lukewarm denominational Sunday school materials for senior adult classes, financial involvement in the Yates Association in partnership with aggressively liberal churches, special Sundays like "Senior Adult Sunday" and "International Sunday," and many other smaller issues too numerous to mention. In other churches, issues may have to do with the decor in the building, music styles (more on that later), annual special events, or traditional patterns that make some constituency in the church happy. A young pastor coming in may have a vision for a more vibrant ministry that leaves behind some of these traditional patterns, but it is best for him to have patience and wait for the right time to address these. Often by the time that issue is finally addressed, almost everyone regularly involved in the church will see the wisdom for the change. There was no "blood spilled" needlessly over an issue that was not critical to the revitalization of the church.

In the end, the Japanese had so heavily fortified Rabaul with more than one hundred thousand troops that naval historian Samuel Eliot Morrison says, "Tarawa, Iwo Jima and Okinawa would have faded to pale pink in comparison with the blood which would have flowed if the Allies had attempted an assault on fortress Rabaul."[2] Those one hundred thousand Japanese soldiers, so intensely prepared for a fight at Rabaul, surrendered peacefully en masse at the end of the war. Church revitalizers should learn when to bypass an issue and wait on the Lord for a peaceful surrender.

"One Blind Eye and One Deaf Ear"

In "Lectures to My Students," Charles Spurgeon advocates that every pastor should have "one blind eye and one deaf ear" and be skilled in knowing when to use them.[3] This goes under the categories of both humility and patience (long-suffering). A pastor who is too thin-skinned and cannot bear patiently the hostility of people who will murmur and complain against what he is trying to do in revitalization will not last long. As Spurgeon said about the poisons of the tongue, "What can't be cured must be endured, and the best way of enduring is not to listen to it."[4] As Proverbs 19:11 puts it, "Good sense makes one slow to anger; it is to his glory to overlook an offense."

PRACTICAL ADVICE

1. Begin with prayer. Recognize that you lack the patience you will need to guide the church step by step through revitalization. Honestly put your impatience before God in prayer every day. Ask that the fruit of the Spirit—including patience—be evident in you.

2. When it comes to bearing patiently with others who are sinning against you, remind yourself constantly through prayer how patient God has been and continues to be with you. Humility and patience with others go together.

3. Study the patience of God in salvation. See how patient God was with Israel's wandering ways. Study in 2 Peter 3 the stated purpose of God's "delaying" the second

coming of Christ—salvation for those who have not yet repented.

4. When it comes to the meat of the Word, remind yourself how long it took you to accept these weightier doctrines. Do not expect others to understand in a week what it took you a lot longer to grasp.

5. Learn to see patience and courage as partners in revitalization, not enemies. There are times for patience, waiting for the congregation to embrace the needed changes. And there are times for bold, courageous leadership. Ask God for the needed wisdom to know what each issue calls for.

6. Think often of the role of patience in your own sanctification. The work of church revitalization is also part of your own journey of salvation. God is not in a hurry to sanctify you. You are like a cake that needs more time in the oven. Bear it patiently!

7. Begin to analyze the different issues that you think need changing for the church to be revitalized. See if there are any issues on the list that are nonessentials, and that, like Rabaul, are worth bypassing for the sake of your reputation and the unity of the church. Give those issues to God in prayer.

8. Build the trust of the congregation by your faithfulness in teaching the Word and your godliness in living it out. When the congregation trusts you, they will follow you.

9. Meditate on the agricultural nature of the parables, including how Mark 4:26–29 shows that there is a prescribed order of growth that cannot be hurried and that God alone can give. Wait on the Lord!

10. Urge patience also in the hearts of your co-laborers in revitalization. From time to time you may have to restrain their immoderate zeal as Martin Luther did with the violent iconoclasts who were ravaging Catholic churches.

12

Be Discerning

A hill to die on." This common phrase refers to an issue or belief that is so important that it is worth fighting for, no matter what the cost. It implies that there are some matters worth dying for and others that are not. It is a military image that pictures the genius of a battlefield commander and his understanding of what ground must be defended at all costs and what must not. For example, when in the Battle of Gettysburg, Joshua Lawrence Chamberlain's 20th Maine Regiment took up their position at the crest of Little Round Top, they were told that they were the extreme left of the Union Army. Chamberlain knew that if the Confederate infantry was able to push past them, they could roll up the entire Union position from the flank and probably win the battle, if not the war. Therefore, he and his regiment fought with a relentless tenacity equal to the critical nature of their position. For Chamberlain and the Union Army, Little Round Top was a hill to die on.

When it comes to church revitalization, a leader's ability to discern what issues are worth fighting for and what are not could mean the difference between success and failure in a particular church. It is important not to draw a line in the sand regarding something not essential to life and godliness. This is a particular fault of young, zealous pastors who yearn to be faithful to God in adverse circumstances, to prove their courage and their willingness to suffer, or perhaps more darkly, to exert their power and authority over any issue in the church.

Are There Nonessentials?

A famous quote falsely attributed to Augustine says, "In essentials, unity; in nonessentials, liberty; in all things, charity." It most likely entered church history during the Thirty Years' War in Germany, a war fought over Christian doctrine, and it has been a favorite of peace lovers and even of some theological liberals who care little for doctrine. I heard a story about a well-known preacher of the Word, a man characterized by boldness and uncompromising clarity in his preaching still to this day, who also tends to allow for no gray areas. Everything is equally true, certain, clear, essential. When he came to his church, that famous quote was painted on the side of the church vans; he had them painted over with the phrase, "There are no nonessentials!" Well, in one sense that famous pastor is right; he is asserting the certainty and seriousness with which we should embrace the Word of God.

That being said, not every issue is worth fighting over—or at least addressing right away. First, not all doctrinal issues are of equal weight. Jesus rebuked the scribes and Pharisees on this very issue: "Woe to you, scribes and Pharisees, hypocrites! For you tithe mint and dill and cumin, and have neglected the weightier matters of the law: justice and mercy and faithfulness. These you ought to have done, without neglecting the others. You blind guides, straining out a gnat and swallowing a camel" (Matt. 23:23–24). Perhaps there are some "gnat" issues and some "camel" issues in church reform; it is essential to discern which is which.[1]

Second, not every church fight is over doctrine. Many are over secondary issues, like finances or the appearance of the church building or for us, the use of projectors and screens in our corporate worship. Many of these issues come down to personal preference and power. Numerous churches split over power struggles, not over doctrine. Save your strength for attacks on the inspiration and authority of the Bible, on the gospel message, on the purity of the church, and on other major issues.

The Need for Discernment

It is clear that we need wisdom from God for all of this. This chapter, in combination with the previous two (on courage and patience), highlights opposite flaws in human character. On the one hand, the coward is tempted to flee when he should stand and fight, to compromise when none should ever be tolerated. On the other hand, the contentious man is tempted to fight about everything that offends him or every personal preference; in reality, he just may be a control freak whose ego forces him to dominate the church. Only

God's gift of wisdom will enable us to avoid these opposite extremes.

Some people think no issue is worth risking church strife over; hence, they will stand for no doctrinal issue—because the unity of the church is most important. But unity must center on doctrine. And even when it is time to fight for a doctrinal issue, we still need wisdom to know how to navigate each particular issue. God has promised to give us wisdom whenever we ask for it. King Solomon admitted that he was young, inexperienced, and did not know how to lead God's people. So he asked for wisdom: "Give your servant therefore an understanding mind to govern your people, that I may discern between good and evil, for who is able to govern this your great people" (1 Kings 3:9). So also James 1:5 says, "If any of you lacks wisdom, let him ask God, who gives generously to all without reproach, and it will be given him."

If some issue surfaces in church revitalization and you do not know whether it is "a hill to die on," ask God for wisdom. Also seek godly counsel from others more experienced in the ministry. "Where there is no guidance, a people falls, but in an abundance of counselors there is safety" (Prov. 11:14). Do not feel embarrassed if you are unable to immediately tell the difference between a vital issue and one worthy of compromise or postponement. Local churches are among the most complex human institutions on the earth.

So Much to Do . . . Where to Begin?!

Any church that has a long history but has in recent years slid toward spiritual death will have myriad dysfunctions that should be addressed. At FBC in 1998, I felt many things needed to be changed. Now that I am seventeen years into my ministry, most of those issues have been addressed. The main issue that FBC ended up fighting over was a doctrinal one: gender and authority. The fight was over whether women could be deacons as we defined the role at the time. I decided to teach not on female deacons per se (which I believe is acceptable biblically, as long as deacons are defined as servants and not authoritative leaders) but on gender and authority. I also discerned the true issue was the role of the Bible in the life of the church: Would we be a church willing to challenge societal norms like feminism and egalitarianism, or would we relegate the Bible to a backseat status?

Related to this issue were several other matters. As I previously mentioned, the entire church polity needed addressing—elders, deacons, committees, congregationalism, et al. Additionally, there were deeper issues of regenerate church membership and a problem of bloated membership rolls. My own inexperience as a pastor and the very short time I had been at FBC had an impact on the way I addressed these issues. For example, what should be handled first?

In other matters, much church reform needed to be done. For instance, the church held an annual patriotic service near the Fourth of July in which Christianity seemed to be subjugated to Americana, especially since a subcommittee of laymen and women ran that "worship service" apart from any input by the pastor. They would tell the pastor what he could and could not preach on or would simply replace him with a pastor of their own choosing. It set a strange precedent for the authority of the pastor in the preaching ministry of the church. That is an example of many traditions in the church that were biblically questionable. The church housed many pictures of Jesus on the walls, as well as plaques and pictures of key members. Church elections for selecting deacons were not done in a way conducive to ensuring that those elected were qualified biblically. The local outreaches were not well organized and resulted in chaos when some children from the inner city were bussed to the church and dropped off on Wednesday evenings for Bible study with no gifted workers trained and ready to receive them. The Wednesday evening prayer supper incorporated very little spirituality: the pastor would give a brief devotional in the fellowship hall while people ate their meals and talked; less than half the people in the room then attended the subsequent prayer time, and carried on murmured conversations the entire time.

Furthermore, a faction of leaders who considered FBC to be "their" church were willing to fight any strong initiatives to turn the ministry more toward biblical faithfulness. For them, almost any pastoral initiative was a threat, and eventually, they would use their influence to run the pastor out.

I could go on and on. Every church revitalization situation has a broad spectrum of issues to address. How to know which ones are vital to the future health of the church is key to wise leadership of any church revitalization effort.

PRACTICAL QUESTIONS TO ASK

1. Does this issue undermine the inspiration and authority of the Bible? In other words, if this issue is not addressed soon, will it send the message that the Bible is no longer the rule of faith and practice in the church?

2. Is the tension behind this issue caused by pride and turf mentality (i.e., people defending aspects of church life they felt belonged especially to them) on the part of church members?

3. Is this issue one of the central pillars of doctrine established in the church's statement of faith? Does it relate to the message of the gospel or how sinners are made right with God or the deity and exclusivity of Christ?

4. Does this issue significantly undermine the church's zeal for and fruitfulness in evangelism in the community?

5. Can this issue be addressed before the church is substantially unified (e.g., church discipline)?

6. Is this issue predominantly a matter of taste and preference, or is it a matter of biblical principle? If the latter, can you cite key scriptural passages that are being violated?

7. Is this issue a matter of tradition and not biblical patterns of church ministry? If it is merely a church tradition, how can you best go about moving to more solid ground before you challenge it? (For example, if the church has been doing a Christmas pageant every year that is ghastly expensive in terms of time, labor, and money—and there is very little spiritual fruit that comes from it—how can you best change hearts and minds, before seeking to challenge the event's future existence?)

8. Is this issue related to the church's decor or spiritual vitality?

9. Is it possible that some of your opponents are unregenerate and that the deeper matter is not the issue itself but their own spiritual health?

10. Have you established a track record of faithful, biblical teaching/leadership on which to draw in order to lead the church through this contentious issue? If not, do that first!

13

Wage War against Discouragement

Imagine what the devil is facing as he seeks to oppose the advance of Christ's kingdom. The Bible says that we Christians, Satan's human enemies, are arrayed with an awesome combination of both offensive and defensive weaponry. In 2 Corinthians 10:3–5, Paul describes our offensive weapons with unforgettable language, saying they have "divine power to destroy strongholds," which are satanic concepts and patterns that oppose the knowledge of God. And there is no defense Satan can erect that can resist the power of those weapons!

In the same way, our defensive armor is fashioned by the hand of God and is perfectly effective, actually *impenetrable* by any weapons Satan can devise. In Ephesians 6:14–17, Paul describes the "whole armor of God," including a breastplate, a helmet, and a "shield of faith," which is so effective it can "extinguish *all* the flaming darts of the evil one" (emphasis mine). When Satan swings his sword of lies and we raise "the sword of the Spirit, which is the word of God," and the swords clash with a resounding crash, we know ours is unbreakable, for "Scripture cannot be broken" (John 10:35), but his weapon will disintegrate! So when we are arrayed in this kind of armor, none of Satan's weapons will do us any harm at all.

So what is the devil to do? His only option is to employ deception: he must lie to us sufficiently before the battle so that, completely demoralized, we *never even get dressed for the battle or pick up a single weapon*. If he can achieve this, he will stand unchallenged in the field while our powerful and skillfully wrought arsenal lies unused on the ground. Satan's top priority in stopping the advance of the church is discouragement.

Reasons Why Church Revitalizers Get Discouraged

All Christians get discouraged from time to time, no matter their ministry. That we are human, with inherent weakness in our hearts and bodies, makes discouragement common. Against the direct Satanic attack I mentioned a moment ago, we are frail, helpless novices compared to the vicious experience of our evil foe. He knows all our weak spots.

Church revitalizers are especially susceptible to spiritual discouragement. Let us start with the discouraging setting of the church. Perhaps the church is in an economically depressed region with a high unemployment rate, resulting in individuals leaving the community to find jobs. Perhaps the church is in a rural area away from a population center. It has not had a visitor in months, while the average age of its members steadily creeps higher. Perhaps the church is in an urban setting in an aging building that has very little appeal to newcomers in the community. Perhaps the church has a poisonous faction of power-hungry leaders who make it their business to oppose any vision for a new direction the pastor may cast. Or perhaps the church is in a nice suburb but saddled with a large debt because of its beautiful new building. Or perhaps it's dying because of a church split five years ago. The challenges facing scenarios like these seem insurmountable.

To make matters worse, all church revitalizations involve some level of internal division and opposition. Personal attacks, questioning of motives, factions and cliques, gossip and slander, anger and finger-pointing, and climactic church votes are almost always issues. There may even be lawsuits or prospective lawsuits (as was the case at FBC). Along with all of this is the fact that God doesn't promise that any local church that has begun a slide toward extinction will at some point reverse course and begin to flourish again. Despite the best efforts of godly people, the end result may be the death of that church.

Even Bible Heroes Became Discouraged

One does not have to look long to find how prevalent spiritual depression is in the Bible. Job said he was in misery, bitter in soul, and longing for death (Job 3:20–21). Jonah yearned for death outside the walls of Nineveh, saying that it was better for him to die than to live (Jon. 4:3). Hannah was overwhelmed with sorrow concerning her continued barrenness and refused to eat (1 Sam. 1:7). King Hezekiah was deeply depressed because of his apparently terminal illness, feeling that God was hunting him down like a lion to break all his bones (Isa. 38:13). Jeremiah was called the weeping prophet, and his personal mourning and anguish reach a peak in Lamentations 3: "My soul is bereft of peace; I have forgotten what happiness is; so I say, 'My endurance has perished; so has my hope from the LORD.' Remember my affliction and my wanderings, the wormwood and the gall. My soul continually remembers it and is bowed down within me" (vv. 17–20). Elijah, the day after his triumph over the prophets of Baal, ran for his life from Queen Jezebel and ended up greatly discouraged: "It is enough; now, O LORD, take away my life, for I am no better than my fathers" (1 Kings 19:4).

In the New Testament, John the Baptist, languishing in Herod's prison for his own execution, sent messengers to Jesus to ask him, "Are you the one who is to come, or shall we look for another?" (Matt. 11:3). *Another?* Someone other than the one he called "the Son of God" (John 1:34), about whom God had testified from heaven and on whom the Holy Spirit had descended in the form of a dove? This can be nothing other than discouragement. And at the end of his amazingly fruitful ministry of church planting and Scripture writing, the apostle Paul said, "All who are in Asia turned away from me" (2 Tim. 1:15).

Most stunning of all is an insight I have gleaned from Isaiah 49:4 about our Lord and Savior, Jesus Christ. That verse is in the middle of an amazing prophecy about the

"Suffering Servant" who would come not only as the Savior of Israel, but also as the "light for the nations" who would bring God's salvation to the ends of the earth (Isa. 49:6). Jesus said through Isaiah, "I have labored in vain; I have spent my strength for nothing and vanity; yet surely my right is with the LORD, and my recompense with my God" (Isa. 49:4). I have come to the conclusion that, in this passage, Jesus was speaking prophetically from the perspective of the cross, similar to "My God, my God, why have you forsaken me?" (Ps. 22:1). So in the dereliction and vast emptiness of the cross, it would have seemed at that moment that his whole life and ministry had been a failure. All of his disciples had deserted him and fled for their lives (Matt. 26:56). Peter had denied him three times. And at the foot of the cross, all that was left after his perfect life of ministry was his mother, a few female friends of the family, and John. "I have labored in vain; I have spent my strength for nothing and vanity." I claim this is only reflective of the *apparent* failure of Christ's ministry. Apparent failure is not the final word—he immediately says "yet." "Yet surely my right is with the LORD, and my recompense with my God" (Isa 49:4). In other words, "Father, into your hands I commit my ministry. Do something with this!" And the Father effectively answers, "Sit at my right hand until I make your name greater than the greatest men in history, and reward you with a multitude of worshipers from every nation on earth!" (see Heb. 1:13).

Every church revitalizer will come to a similar place in the work: "I have labored to no purpose. I have spent my strength in vain and for nothing." It is vital at that moment to entrust your life and ministry into the same hands that Jesus did—the omnipotent and loving hands of our heavenly Father.

Across the Ages

Church history is full of accounts of mighty servants of God who struggled for a time in the "slough of despond."[1] Charles Spurgeon, the great nineteenth-century Baptist preacher, was among them. Despite leading thousands of people around the world to saving faith in Christ, he regularly battled depression. In his *Lectures to My Students* is a chapter titled "The Minister's Fainting Fits," which addresses this very issue. He writes, "Fits of depression come over the most of us. Usually cheerful as we may be, we must at intervals be cast down. The strong are not always vigorous, the wise not always ready, the brave not always courageous, and the joyous not always happy."[2] Spurgeon included himself: "Knowing by most painful experience what deep depression of spirit means, being visited therewith at seasons by no means few and far between."[3]

Church history contains many such stories:

- *Martin Luther*. He was so dejected about the poor progress of the gospel in Wittenberg that he gave up preaching for fifteen months in 1529–30.[4] Spurgeon writes that Luther's "great spirit was often in the seventh heaven of exultation, and as frequently on the borders of despair."[5]

- *Hudson Taylor*. He was a nineteenth-century missionary to China whom God used to lead tens of thousands of Chinese to Christ. After a riot in Yangchow caused financial support to dwindle and opposition to increase, he wrote in 1875 to his sister of his discouragement reaching the level of despair: "I prayed, agonized, fasted, strove, made resolutions, read the Word more diligently, sought more time for meditation—but all without avail."[6]

- *Adoniram Judson*. After the death of his beloved wife, Ann, the nineteenth-century missionary to Burma, who had seen no converts, fell into a deep depression. He built a hut out in the jungle and behind it dug his own grave, spending hours staring into it, contemplating his own death. He writes, "God is to me the Great Unknown. I believe in him, but I find him not."[7] God was gracious to Judson, rescuing him gradually from despair and enabling him eventually to lead thousands to Christ. But not without a mighty battle against depression.

- *William Cowper*. The nineteenth-century hymn writer (author of "Praise for the Fountain Opened," also known by its first line, "There is a fountain filled with blood") wrote this in a letter to John Newton: "Loaded as my life is with despair, I have no such comfort as would result from a supposed probability of better things to come, were it once ended. . . . You will tell me that this cold gloom will be succeeded by a cheerful spring, and endeavour to encourage me to hope for a spiritual change resembling it—but it will be lost labour."[8]

- *David Brainerd*. An eighteenth-century missionary to Native Americans, Brainerd's journal entry for December 16, 1744, reads: "Was so overwhelmed with dejection that I knew not how to live: I longed for death exceedingly: My soul was 'sunk in deep waters,' and 'the floods' were ready to 'drown me.' I was so much oppressed that my soul was in a kind of horror."[9]

- *A. B. Simpson.* The founder of the Christian and Missionary Alliance writes, "I fell into the slough of despond so deep that . . . work was impossible . . . I wandered about deeply depressed. All things in life looked dark and withered."[10]

All these heroes for Christ accomplished great things amid battles with depression. Satan was slinging all the flaming arrows he could at these choice servants of the Lord to keep them from damaging his dark kingdom any more than they already had.

Preach Yourself Out of Spiritual Depression

Perhaps the most important sermons you will ever hear are those you preach to yourself when your soul is sliding down the slope of depression. D. Martyn Lloyd-Jones wrote a classic book on this subject entitled *Spiritual Depression: Its Causes and Cure.* The central text of the book is from Psalm 42:5, 11: "Why are you cast down, O my soul, and why are you in turmoil within me? Hope in God; for I shall again praise him, my salvation." Just as the psalmist rebukes his own soul over the gloom that has cast it down, reasoning with himself that God is still worthy of praise, so Lloyd-Jones makes this observation:

> Have you realized that most of your unhappiness in life is due to the fact that you are listening to yourself instead of talking to yourself? . . . The main art in the matter of spiritual living is to know how to handle yourself. You have to take yourself in hand, you have to address yourself, preach to yourself, question yourself. You must say to your soul, 'Why art thou cast

down?' What business have you to be disquieted? You must turn on yourself, upbraid yourself, condemn yourself, exhort yourself, and say to yourself, 'Hope thou in God' instead of muttering in this depressed, unhappy way. And then, you must go on to remind yourself of God, who God is, what God has done, and what God has pledged himself to do.[11]

My Lowest Point and How Psalm 37 Rescued Me

My journey toward church revitalization at FBC reached its lowest point just before a climactic church conference that would decide the doctrinal issue over which we had been fighting. The Sunday before that church conference was the hardest day of preaching in my almost seventeen years of ministry at FBC. The tension was so thick I could barely catch my breath or walk steadily to preach. The text was not a particularly difficult passage, but I was preaching to so many hate-filled faces that I found myself clutching the sides of the pulpit just to keep upright. After barely making it through that sermon, I went home to recuperate for the evening service. I lay down in a hammock out in the backyard and prayed . . . and cried.

As I lay there, I felt I was at the breaking point and could not take much more. A godly church member had recommended that morning that I read Psalm 37 for encouragement. That afternoon, I did. Line after line of this ancient psalm washed over my heart and eased my burdens. I felt as though God himself were speaking those words to me. The basic point of the psalm is stated right at the beginning: "Fret not yourself because of evildoers; be not envious of wrongdoers! For they will soon fade like the grass and wither like the green herb. Trust in the LORD, and do good; dwell in the land and befriend faithfulness" (vv. 1–3). The clear message kept coming across in the Psalm: wicked people make plots and schemes against the righteous, but they will fail. In the end, the righteous will inherit the earth, and the wicked will be no more. So do not fret or be anxious, do not worry or be alarmed. Simply stand firm and watch the deliverance that God will bring about. God even comforted me about a potential lawsuit I had heard some of my opponents were planning: "The wicked watches for the righteous and seeks to put him to death. The LORD will not abandon him to his power or let him be condemned when he is brought to trial" (vv. 32–33).

Two verses especially resonated with me: "I have seen a wicked, ruthless man, spreading himself like a green laurel tree. But he passed away, and behold, he was no more; though I sought him, he could not be found" (vv. 35–36). This made such an impression on my heart that I rose out of my hammock, got a saw, and cut off a leafy green branch from a tree. As soon as the saw passed through that branch, the leaves were dead, though there was no appearance of the fact—they looked as leafy and healthy as they had a moment before. But soon the leaves would inevitably wither because they were cut off from the living source. I took that branch with me to work, and I still have it. The leaves are completely dead now, because I cut the branch nearly fifteen years ago. It represents the end of the era of unregenerate church members dominating the life of FBC.

That time of meditation and prayer completely changed my perspective in less than an hour. I knew immediately what would happen at that climactic Wednesday night church conference: the plots and schemes of the powerful men who opposed me would succeed in the short term, but the church would be healthy in the long term. In common language, we would lose the battle at the church conference but win the war for church revitalization. I went to work as usual on Monday morning, but the staff all saw a noticeable change in my demeanor. I was happy, confident, and excited about what was going to happen long term at FBC. Everyone around me relaxed as well—and waited to see what God would do. As I look back on all this, I now realize that my time of prayerful meditation on Psalm 37 was a pivotal moment in the entire church reform. If I had continued in my depression, and the vote had turned out as it did, I almost certainly would have resigned and taken another pastorate that was then being offered to me. I wonder if FBC would have been reformed at that point. God could have raised up someone else to lead, but the same battle still would have needed to be fought.

PRACTICAL ADVICE

1. Expect Satan to attack you with discouragement often during the journey of church revitalization.

2. Make a list of all the challenges that face you in church revitalization: issues, obstacles, people, events, etc. Spread that list out before the Lord often in prayer, as did Hezekiah in Isaiah 37. Cast "all your anxieties on him, because he cares for you" (1 Pet. 5:7).

3. Gather people around you for prayer and encouragement. Lean on friends when discouragement starts to come in like waves and breakers.

4. Use the book of Psalms often. There is no emotional state in life and ministry that some psalm does not accurately capture. Let the psalmists speak for you to God and from God to you.

5. Preach to yourself. Often. Use Psalm 42:11 to reason with yourself.

6. Humble yourself under God's mighty hand. Recognize that you are a sinner saved by grace whom God chooses to use for his purposes. Don't make too much of your earthly happiness or ministry success.

7. Remind yourself that God has not promised to revitalize your church, but he has promised to raise from the dead all of Christ's sheep so that not one of them will be lost (John 6:39–40, 44, 54).

8. Go for a walk in nature or take a vacation to the mountains or the sea. Breathe the air. Look at the scenery. Walk through the woods. Smell the musty smell of the forest. Pick a flower and look at it carefully.

9. Read Lloyd-Jones's *Spiritual Depression* and follow its prescriptions. Do the same with Charles Spurgeon's "The Minister's Fainting Fits," which is available for free download online.

10. Combat your depression with praise and Scripture meditation. Sing triumphant hymns of worship. Read clear promises of God's everlasting presence and omnipotence. Especially read Isaiah 40 and renew your vision of almighty God, sitting enthroned above the circle of the earth, its people like grasshoppers. Wait on the Lord, and you will mount up with wings as eagles,

you will run and not be weary, and you will walk and not be faint (Isa. 40:31).

11. Be careful not to reveal your discouragement too openly to those who consider you a leader. If you need confidants, choose those who are strong in the faith, perhaps even some pastors from other churches. Do not be a source of discouragement to the weaker and more immature who are looking to you for leadership.

14

Develop and Establish Men as Leaders

would not still be pastor of FBC if God had not graciously given me some men as fellow warriors for the revitalization of our church. Some of those men were at FBC when I arrived and had been praying for years that God would transform their beloved church. Others were called by God to join after my arrival. Without their courageous and sacrificial leadership, I would have been evicted from my ministry long ago. No one can revitalize a church alone. God must raise up godly men to strive together in the work, or it will inevitably fail.

Inspect the Rubble First, Then Gather Leaders

What are the first steps a pastor should take in revitalization? Perhaps Nehemiah is a pattern to follow. Nehemiah was burdened with a passion for the glory of God and the good of his people. He received a report from his brother Hanani concerning the lamentable condition of the city of Jerusalem, which was little more than a pile of rubble, stripped of all defenses because its wall had been demolished. Jeremiah was cupbearer to the Persian king, who ruled the mightiest empire that region of the world had ever seen, and was in a position to ask for the resources necessary to attempt the rebuilding project. Having pleaded with God for grace and having received the grant of resources from the king, Nehemiah traveled to Jerusalem to begin this massive undertaking.

My counsel for the first steps of revitalization begins with Nehemiah's actions when he arrived in Jerusalem (Neh. 2). First, he rested from his journey for three days. This is reasonable, for we don't make wise decisions when we're weary. Correspondingly, when a pastor first comes to a church, he needs time to settle. He also enjoys a brief "honeymoon period" with the church (mine did not last too long!) in which he is acclimated into ministry there.

Next, Nehemiah took a few men along with him on a secret nighttime tour of the city walls. Nehemiah is very clear that he kept hidden what God had laid on his heart to do for Jerusalem. This is also an extremely important aspect of the revitalization work of a new pastor. He hopefully has come in with a clear vision of what a healthy church looks like, both in doctrine and in life. Nehemiah kept his thoughts to himself, but he led these few men around with him to see the condition of the entire circuit of Jerusalem's city wall. This corresponds to a pastor beginning to bring other men in on his inspection of the church and its condition. He may ask these men questions about the preaching that went on before he came, about the Sunday school program or other educational ministries of the church, the outreach patterns, the social life, the organization. They are metaphorically "riding around the walls at night," seeing the condition of the dying church with new eyes.

Having completed his inspection, Nehemiah unburdened his mind to the leaders who would be instrumental in doing the work—the priests, nobles, and officials:

> "You see the trouble we are in, how Jerusalem lies in ruins with its gates burned. Come, let us build the wall of Jerusalem, that we may no longer suffer derision." And I told them of the hand of my God that had been upon me for good, and also of the words that the king had spoken to me. And they said, "Let us rise up and build." So they strengthened their hands for the good work. (Neh. 2:17–18)

I love this example of visionary leadership by Nehemiah! It was obviously impossible for him by himself to rebuild the wall of Jerusalem out of massive piles of rubble. Yet it was only after he had made a careful inspection of the actual scope of the problems with his own eyes that Nehemiah was ready to involve other leaders with him. No leader, no matter how visionary, can revitalize a dying church alone. He must involve other men as leaders with him. But he must do so wisely, after he has inspected the spiritual "rubble" of the church for himself.

Early Stages: Gathering Key Men to Pray

Practically speaking, I would recommend a new pastor begin his ministry by praying daily through the church directory. This is a habit that should continue as long as he is a pastor, not just when the church needs revitalizing. He should especially be seeking like-minded men who could be future leaders in the effort at church renewal. He should quietly be "inspecting the walls," talking to men about their lives, their doctrine, their dreams for the church. He is seeking key co-laborers who will join with him in the challenging journey ahead. He does not need these men to be copiously trained theologically or to be fully mature leaders, but they need to be born again, living for Christ, loving God's Word, and eager to learn.

When the time is right, he should begin gathering these men together for focused prayer times. These gatherings are the beginning of the plurality of elders in that church, if that church has never had that biblical pattern of leadership before. All of these early prayer partners will not necessarily be qualified as elders or established in that office. However, the strength that comes from these hand-selected men will be invaluable for the often difficult journey ahead. Imagine how beneficial it would be to have men to pray with you and give you counsel before a climactic church vote on a key issue. Think of the value of having men who will hold you accountable to respond to bitter enemies with kindness and love, or who will be willing to have difficult conversations with folks so you don't always have to do it yourself. And beyond this is simply the power of united prayer, of pouring out your hearts together for the transformation of the church.

Communicating the Vision

Such gatherings of key men are where you can also begin doing solid biblical instruction on elements of a healthy church—

what it is you want to see that church become. You can root these elements in Scripture and persuade the men that this is what Christ wants his church to be. Just as Nehemiah held his peace until the right time and then communicated the vision to the leaders, so you should do with your hand-selected men. If any of them push back or disagree, be patient and keep instructing. Prove your argument using Scripture, and they will join you in the work—if they are in fact Spirit-filled men. If not, they will not want to keep meeting and praying with you.

Male Leadership

Let me offer a brief word regarding male leadership of the church. In all successful church revitalization situations, God will certainly raise up godly women who will be absolutely vital in the work. They will have many invaluable, God-given spiritual gifts for the blessing of the church. They will pray fervently, offer wise counsel, serve tirelessly, offer hospitality, and instruct other women if they have teaching gifts. But God has reserved the leadership of both the family and the church to men. This was the very issue FBC was fighting over during our journey of revitalization. The biblical proof of this is found in key Scriptures like 1 Timothy 2:12, which says, "I do not permit a woman to teach or to exercise authority over a man; rather, she is to remain quiet." Churches are blessed with godly, humble, and Christlike male leaders who honor women and treat them with respect but do not shirk their duty to lead as Adam did in the garden of Eden.[1]

Let Another Mouth Defend You

One of the great benefits of a new pastor gathering a group of godly men will be evidenced once things start to get "hot," once the false accusations start to fly. Satan will raise up powerful opposition to the revitalization of the church "from among your own selves" (Acts 20:30), and the fight may get pretty dirty. The insults and accusations that came my way during those years were amazing! But if you have a group of godly men around you who know your heart, see your vision, and recognize your humble example, they will be motivated to stand up for you. Proverbs 27:2 says, "Let another praise you, and not your own mouth; a stranger, and not your own lips." In the same way, "Let another *defend* you, and not your own mouth; a stranger, and not your own lips." If the attack is at you and not at the issue, let someone else defend it.

In the same way, these godly men will be ready to confront you if they think you are doing anything wrong. I remember two of the men in my support group confronted me about a tone of pride they had heard in one of my recent sermons. They were right; I repented and asked their forgiveness. They prayed for me. This is the rich benefit of having a group of men around you when working to revive a dying church.

The Goal for Leadership: Plural Elders

In 1998, FBC had five points of power, and it was unclear how each should relate to one another in the governance of the church. These were the five:

(1) *Senior pastor and staff.* The senior pastor was responsible for directing the paid staff and leading the focus of the

church's ministries. He was "checked and balanced" by the deacons and the committees.

(2) *Board of deacons.* The deacons were elected annually by a church election and were tasked with generally overseeing the life of the church in partnership with the pastor. However, the deacons were not filtered by spiritual criteria in 1 Timothy 3:8–13; names were written on a nominating ballot, the nominating committee contacted them to see if they were willing to run, and the eight with the highest votes were elected. The vote tallies were tabulated and retained, and the one with the next highest vote was named an alternate. In case any deacon that year needed to resign, that alternate would step into the role. Many key deacons sought to control church life by controlling the important committees.

(3) *Church committees.* The church had many committees (more than I can remember), but some of the most influential were nominating, budget and finance, personnel, building and grounds, and missions. The nominating committee was the most powerful in a sense—because they identified the chairs of each of these committees, who generally controlled those committees. The budget and finance held the purse strings. Some FBC pastors before me told me that key financial givers would control the "financial health" of the church by withholding their giving to make the pastor look bad. The personnel committee (where is that in the Bible?) considered themselves the supervisors of the pastor and all paid staff. They gave annual performance reviews for the pastor and controlled salary increases.

(4) *Church council.* Made up of the chairs of all the committees (including minor ones, like the flower committee),

this odd group felt it had the power to make key decisions pertaining to the life and direction of the church, which the pastor had to abide by.

(5) *The congregation.* As in any Baptist church, the congregation was the final and highest human authority. It voted on all key issues and initiatives, especially at bimonthly church conferences. These meetings were run democratically according to *Robert's Rules of Order.* But they were often quite contentious and easily manipulated by "getting out the vote" and by the "old-boy network" of influence and relational pull. Many votes were rubber stamps of what the key committee chairs wanted done.

This hodgepodge of lines of influence and competing areas of power was a confusing, unbiblical mess. Beyond this came the problem of a prideful "turf warfare" in which various factions would defend their areas with sinful pride. Servant leadership in the pattern of Matthew 20:25–28 was the remedy Jesus commanded for this kind of pride and self-interest. God established a better pattern in the pages of the New Testament in the plurality of elders. I began mentioning the desire I had to move to this pattern in my initial interviews with the pastoral search committee, but it would be a long time before we could see it come to fruition.

The biblical case for plural elders is made plain in Titus 1:5: "This is why I left you in Crete, so that you might put what remained into order, and appoint elders in every town as I directed you." One town, one church, plural elders. We see the same in Acts 14:23: "And when [Paul and Barnabas] had appointed elders for them in every church, with prayer and fasting they committed them to the Lord, in whom they had believed." Again, plural elders in each church.

The key issue with elders[2] is the spiritual criteria used to filter these men and make certain they are fit for the office as it is taught clearly in Titus 1:6–9 and 1 Timothy 3:1–7.

Many churches think pastors are always paid professionals who have a degree from seminary and that the only role for lay leaders is that of deacon. In actuality, deacons in the New Testament are never portrayed as having authority or as being leaders. They are servants tasked with practical responsibilities under the elders. Lay leaders who meet the biblical criteria of elder should be elected by the congregation and established with equal responsibility and authority as the senior pastor.

The wisdom of God in establishing this plural leadership is amazing. These men can hold one another accountable, support one another in times of conflict, rebuke and correct one another, and see their varying gifts employed to maximize the ministry of the church. "A threefold cord is not quickly broken" (Eccles. 4:12), but at FBC, we have ten elders. A cord of ten strands all united, all leading the church sweetly and lovingly in the same direction, is especially difficult to break.

A Pipeline of Godly Men

A healthy church will have a regular pipeline of godly men being raised up to do the work of shepherding and leading the church. First Timothy 3:1 addresses this: "The saying is trustworthy: If anyone aspires to the office of overseer, he desires a noble task." In other words, for any man to be an overseer is a godly ambition. Even if they never "make it," especially because God does not give them the gift of teaching, the yearning for growth in all the key areas is a godly one and will produce much good fruit in a man's life. If it is true that it is a godly ambition for a man to be an elder, then by extension it must be a healthy thing for a church to develop a pipeline of godly men in training to be leaders at some point. The more mature a church is, the more meticulously planned their spiritual leadership development pattern will be.

Now, a church in the early stages of revitalization will not have anything like this up and running. Nonetheless, the communication of this as the future of the church will inspire godly men to rise up, and godly women to pray for it and help influence husbands and sons toward this end. The church will rise and fall with its leaders.

PRACTICAL ADVICE

1. If you are a pastor, begin praying immediately for God to raise up future elders to share with you in revitalization.

2. Pray regularly through the church directory, asking God to show you the men he is preparing for this role.

3. Early on in the revitalization effort, begin having heartfelt conversations with men who come up to encourage you after sermons or Bible studies. Follow up with these men and see if they possess more spiritual depth than merely a desire to encourage you.

4. Begin looking for a group of men who can gather around you and pray with you and for you. As God starts to raise these men up, ask them if they would be willing to pray with you for the future of the church.

5. Do not overwhelm these men early on; gradually impart the vision God has laid on your heart. Have them

read books with you on elements of healthy church life. *Nine Marks of a Healthy Church* by Mark Dever is an excellent starting point.

6. Begin speaking to more and more people, in wider and wider forums, about God's pattern of plural eldership.

7. Expect turf battles from resistant people. Do not be surprised when those battles occur. Do not lower yourself to act in the same way; rather, be patient and humble.

8. Teach often on servant leadership from the Gospels. Share Christ's teaching in Matthew 20:25–28 and example in John 13:1–10 and Philippians 2:6–9. Seek to live this out yourself.

9. If your bylaws allow you, let others lead at contentious meetings. The bylaws at FBC allowed either the senior pastor or the chairman of the deacons to run our church conferences. As things got heated, it became wiser to let the chairman run the meetings if he was supportive of my ministry. This way it is evident that it is not just you who has this vision of church revitalization.

10. At key church meetings, be sure your people are ready to speak and to vote. In a democratically run church, I often say that history is made by those who show up. Make sure godly people are not absent or silent.

11. When the time is right, push hard for a transformation of your church polity to plural elders. Teach patiently, groom men to be ready for the role. Show that it is biblical. You will need a whole new constitution and bylaws, so study those done by other healthy churches that have plural elders in place. The change will be a significant milestone in your journey of revitalization.

15

Become Supple on Worship

Truly, the sun never sets on the kingdom of Jesus Christ.[1] As the sun runs its circuit through twenty-four time zones every Sunday, it shines down on a countless multitude of people from almost every tribe, language, and nation worshiping the risen Christ. The patterns of worship are as varied as the cultures that wake up every Sunday morning to assemble. I have worshiped with Christian brothers and sisters under a tree in the Rift Valley in Kenya, in a high-rise apartment in Shanghai, in an ornate cathedral in Dresden, and in our Greek Renaissance-style building in Durham. All these worship services had some similarities and some differences. Regardless, the goal has always been the same: to worship God the Father through Christ the Son in the power of the Holy Spirit.

As we consider worship in a church revitalization situation, we come to one of the most painful and contentious issues that church leaders ever face—music. The power of music and the memories it evokes can make worship style "sacred ground" on which a new pastor is hardly allowed to tread. An ironclad grip on particular songs or styles has often caused a widening gap between churches and the surrounding world they are commanded to reach for Christ. It has also caused increasing distance between older and younger Christians who are eager to live for Christ and reach the lost. A church can become frozen in time, clinging to the remnants of a bygone era when the church was the largest in town and all was right with the world. The result can be that the church's membership generally gets older and older as time goes by.

If such a church is to be revitalized, it must repent of its selfishness and become supple in worship, willing to be stretched into new patterns for the sake of the young and the lost. If it refuses to do so, it will simply get older and die. And many churches have done precisely that.

Supple . . . Like New Cloth and New Wineskins

Jesus told a twin parable to teach us this lesson:

> No one puts a piece of unshrunk cloth on an old garment, for the patch tears away from the garment, and a worse tear is made. Neither is new wine put into old wineskins. If it is, the skins burst and the wine is spilled and the skins are destroyed. But new wine is put into fresh wineskins, and so both are preserved. (Matt. 9:16–17)

Both the new cloth and the new wineskins have the same attribute of flexibility that can yield properly to surrounding circumstances. But the old cloth and the old wineskins are set in their ways and cannot respond to the changing circumstance. Because of their lack of flexibility, a catastrophic rupture results.

When applied to church revitalization, this lesson is a powerful one. From within the church will come the transformation of hearts that are newly bursting for the glory of God and the spread of his kingdom. This will put a constant pressure on the church to change its patterns, to rethink everything in the new light of the gospel. This pressure will especially be felt among the young and those who are eager to reach the lost with the gospel. If that dynamic for change hits a wall of inflexibility, a rupture is sure to come. If out of selfishness and sentimentalism, older, wealthier, longer-tenured members say no to changes pertaining to Sunday morning worship, the revitalization will come to a halt.

Timeless and Temporary

At FBC, that pressure for change was happening among our elders and other visionary leaders. They were saying we were not appealing to young, energetic Christians who loved many aspects of FBC church life but felt a strong disconnect with the pipe organ and robed choir that characterized our worship. If we were to have a future, these young, gifted, energetic, and missions-minded Christians were it, and we were losing them week after week.

A key moment came when I preached on the "timeless and temporary" aspects of worship and of gospel ministry in Hebrews 12:28–29. The author of Hebrews writes of the final removing of temporal things—the present heaven and earth—so that the eternal kingdom of Christ might be finally established at the end of all things. He then writes of our present worship of the living God, commanding that we worship God "acceptably," for "our God is a consuming fire." The timeless aspects of God's nature and of the role we have as the redeemed church to worship God are powerfully established. But the whole book of Hebrews was centered on the removal of the outward trappings of the old covenant worship. The animal sacrificial system and the temple priesthood were declared obsolete and would soon disappear (Heb. 8:13). No generation in church history has had to embrace so much radical change in worship patterns as did that generation of Jewish Christians. They had to let go of deeply beloved patterns of worship—the annual pilgrimages to Jerusalem, animal sacrifices, circumcision, and dietary regulations. Those temporary things were being replaced by a new pattern of worship based on the new covenant in Jesus Christ.

The full ramifications of this new pattern of worship would not be clear for decades, but Hebrews was instrumental in making this distinction between timeless and temporary. The timeless aspects of the Christian faith must never be changed: biblical truth about God, humanity, Christ, the gospel, repentance and faith, heaven and hell, etc. Any church that changes these timeless truths to please a disapproving world has signed its own death warrant. So also the church must staunchly maintain timeless New Testament patterns of worship broadly defined, such as the preaching of the Word; the singing of psalms, hymns, and spiritual songs; public prayer; the collection of funds for the work of the church; the right exercise of the ordinances of baptism and Lord's Supper; and the fellowship of the saints.

However, there are also temporary patterns of worship, like animal sacrifice, annual pilgrimages, Gregorian chants, pipe organs, choir robes, and the use of "Just as I Am" at an "invitational" at the end of the sermon, etc. Not only is it true that these temporary things may change, I am arguing here that they *must* change! If a local church clings to a certain cultural pattern of worship and refuses to adapt and be flexible, it will eventually become extinct.

Seeker Sensible, Not Seeker Sensitive

I was concerned that FBC, in changing its worship style, not be motivated by a desire to pander to the tastes of unconverted people. My concern was caused by the doctrinal laxness I saw in many churches that followed the Willow Creek model of being "seeker sensitive."[2] These churches changed whatever they could about the church experience to make it appealing to the lost. A key text for them was 1 Corinthians 9:22, "I have become all things to all people, that by all means I might save some."

Unfortunately, some of the practitioners of this model went too far. I heard once of a lead pastor publicly apologizing to the assembly on Sunday morning that one of their newer worship leaders had used so many "blood" hymns in his song selection. When church leaders begin apologizing for the blood of Christ, they have gone too far in being "sensitive." Timeless aspects must remain and be clearly proclaimed, especially the cross of Jesus Christ. The seeker-sensitive approach directs its attention on Sunday mornings, humanly speaking, primarily toward the lost visitors and not to the Christians. This does not line up with Scripture, which makes the assembly of the church on the Lord's Day an act of worship, instruction, and fellowship among believers to which outsiders are welcome.

Conversely, churches have gone too far in the opposite direction, focusing exclusively on making the church members happy and not caring what outsiders think. At FBC, we have come to embrace a different phrase for corporate worship: "seeker sensible." The key passage for us is 1 Corinthians 14:23–25, in which Paul regulates the speaking of tongues in the Corinthian assembly. Paul was concerned that if they spoke in tongues with no one to interpret and if an outsider should come in and hear what was going on, he would say they were out of their minds. But if they were prophesying (clearly proclaiming the intelligible word of the Lord in a powerful, Spirit-led way) and an unbeliever were to come in, he would be convicted that he is a sinner and would fall down and worship God, exclaiming, "Surely God is among you!" That is the essence of seeker sensibility: the service needs to "make sense" to outsiders, being easily understood, so that the Word of God can have convicting power. But the service still has its primary human focus on the regenerate members, feeding them so they will worship God acceptably with reverence and awe.

Churches in need of revitalization frequently have become so inwardly focused that they do not know or care how they look to their lost neighbors. They assume that the worship patterns they have been using for decades are every bit as beneficial now as they were years ago. A leader who desires to revitalize such a church has a long uphill climb to change that attitude. But it must be done if the church is to survive and, what is more to the point, to thrive.

A Quick Tour Back in Time and around the World

Some of the staunch advocates of continuing to do what they have always done in worship need to get out more! They need to go back in time and around the world to see how their brothers and sisters in other settings have sought to worship the living God. A quick tour of twenty centuries of Christian worship will leave a clear impression of constant change in the "temporary" trappings of corporate worship. The patterns of worship of Christians in the second-century Roman catacombs were very different from what we do on Sunday mornings. For one thing, the early church rejected the use of musical instruments, such as organs, cymbals, and pipes as "childish."[3] After Constantine's conversion to Christianity in AD 325, the church became wealthier, and the construction of costly church buildings commenced in earnest and hasn't stopped yet. In the ninth century, Gregorian chants entered the Western church and were dominant in worship for centuries. The sixteenth-century reformer Ulrich Zwingli in Zurich espoused a very simple worship style focused exclusively on what was commanded in the New Testament. This became known as the "regulative principle," that only those things clearly commanded in the New Testament should be permitted in the church's corporate worship life. Conversely, Martin Luther and many who followed his patterns espoused the "normative principle," that Christians can employ anything in worship not forbidden by Scripture. Luther's love for music gave birth to a German culture of worship, leading to church composers like Johann Sebastian Bach.

After the Reformation, the amazing variety of what brothers and sisters in Christ thought glorified God unfolded. The Puritans in England during the sixteenth and seventeenth centuries only chanted psalms with no musical instruments, but Isaac Watts scandalized many of his generation by setting these psalms to verse in the pattern of English poetry. Some of the stricter sorts in the English church scene considered his hymns "too worldly." Many in the seeker-sensitive movement today would reject them for the opposite reason! In the eighteenth century, John and Charles Wesley filled their Methodist worship services with many new hymns. Our church's Baptist hymnals reflect our country's frontier revivalist heritage—hymns the elderly in our churches are grieving because the younger folks no longer want to sing them. It especially fascinates me that our church struggled with no longer using the pipe organ in favor of more modern instruments like electric guitars and drums. The pipe organ itself was a technological marvel when it was invented, yet organs were removed from churches by the Puritans, who saw them as worldly remnants of sensual Roman Catholic worship.[4]

In the same way, a quick tour around the world to churches on every continent on the earth today should greatly expand the horizons of church traditionalists. They would hear the sounds of our brothers and sisters singing in Africa, Asia, Latin America, Europe, and North America in a variety of ways so wide and rich it would stun their senses. The "timeless" truths of Christianity are being celebrated in a staggering array of "temporary" patterns. To mandate one unchanging pattern is to display ignorance and hinder the transformation of a church that will die if it remains stubborn.

A Key Precept and Its Corollary

From this tour back in time and around the world, I came to a key precept: *God likes more forms of worship than you do.* Along with that came a helpful corollary: *it is good for you to worship in forms that you do not like—but that God does.* To reject the first precept takes a level of arrogance that few people would willingly embrace. To say, "No, God and I are on exactly the same page regarding worship!" is as prideful as it is repugnant. And yet so many church members seem to live out that attitude when it comes to worship. The corollary is helpful to those who can expand their souls to accept the original—if God likes more patterns of worship than I do, it will be good for me to stretch myself and start embracing some new things. "Let each of you look not only to his own interests, but also to the interests of others" (Phil. 2:4).

As a revitalizing leader, it would be good to instruct your church on the history of worship back in time and around the world. Challenge them to expand the temporary trimmings of their own worship to be more attractive to young, energetic Christians and to lost people in the community. Of course, do all of this without ever compromising the timeless things of the Word of God.

Senior Saints Who Help the Cause

Essential to the healthy transformation of a church from dying to thriving are senior saints who embrace these principles and are willing to stretch themselves for the sake of the future. In effect, these godly brothers and sisters need to "take one for the team." No temporary pattern of worship is essential to the gospel—that is why it is in the temporary category. The more modern styles of Christian contemporary music are no more essential than the old styles of "In the Garden" and "Just as I Am." The new is no more valid than the old. But what ends up happening is that the young simply "vote with their feet" and stop coming to that church. Having some senior adults who see that writing on the wall and are willing to sacrifice personal preference that their church will still live long after they die is selfless, godly, and commendable. They are also instrumental in persuading others of their generation that such changes *must* happen or the church will die. Those arguments are much more persuasive coming from peers than from the new young pastor who is saying the same things.

A young revitalizing leader would do well to win some key senior adult leaders to his cause through patient persuasion and careful instruction. He will be calling on some dear people to make sacrifices in order for the church to thrive. What is at stake is the essential difference between a church plant and a revitalization: namely, a multigenerational congregation. Putting up with worship styles you do not love (yet) causes you to deny yourself for the sake of the work of Christ. Sadly, many older church members are not so mature and clamor the loudest for their rights and tastes. As one

195

godly senior man said at FBC, "Their favorite hymn is, 'Have *mine* own way, Lord, have *mine* own way!'" If they remain stubborn, the revitalization will founder on this rock.

PRACTICAL ADVICE

1. As soon as you get to the church, begin praying for the worship service to be passionate and powerful. Worship "in spirit and truth" (John 4:24).

2. If there is an existing worship leader, seek to befriend him and develop a good working relationship with him. You want this worship leader gladly on your page, if possible.

3. Do your own personal study of worship across the ages and around the world. Get familiar with the variety of ways God's people have worshiped him.

4. Ask the Lord to develop your own healthy convictions on this issue. My heart needed change on this as much as did others'.

5. Learn what forms of worship are being used effectively by other healthy and growing churches in your area.

6. Begin praying for God to raise up gifted, talented musicians to enrich your corporate worship. The more skillfully the people play, the greater the blessing for the congregation.

7. Be patient in making changes. Wait until other key things have been established. This is not the top priority when you arrive; but it will almost certainly need to happen for the church to be fully revitalized.

8. When the time is right, begin teaching your prayer partners and other key leaders on the need to become flexible in worship. Ask for their input.

9. If young, energetic Christians are coming to your service, connect with them immediately and get their honest feedback on the worship style at your church. Listen to them. Do not make promises, but give them a long-range vision of what you would like to see happen at the church. Try to win their patience, loyalty, and help.

10. When the time comes to make changes in the worship service, seek to communicate clearly to the church what you want to do and why. Though not everyone will agree, at least they will not feel blindsided.

11. Teach the church the "timeless and temporary" distinction. The "temporary" *must* be constantly developing. But the "timeless" *must never* change.

16

Embrace the Two Journeys of Disciple-Making

Why did Christ leave us here on Earth? Given that we are all in constant spiritual danger from the world, the flesh, and the devil, and given that he will someday rescue us from the present evil age (Gal. 1:4), why doesn't he do it now? We know that, just as Christ created (Isa. 43:7) and redeemed (Eph. 1:12) us for his glory, he also left us in this world for his glory. But how can we glorify God? Jesus showed us that, just as he glorified God on Earth by finishing the work God gave him to do (John 17:4), so must we.

And what is that? Well, all four of the Gospels record some version of what has become known as "The Great Commission." The most famous of these is in Matthew 28:19–20: "Go therefore and make disciples of all nations, baptizing them in the name of the Father and of the Son and of the Holy Spirit, teaching them to observe all that I have commanded you." Making disciples to the ends of the world and to the end of time is the work he left us to do. A disciple is a whole-life learner, someone who is conformed to both the doctrine and lifestyle of the master. The Great Commission involves not only bringing people to that initial moment of saving faith but also teaching them wholehearted obedience to *everything* Christ has commanded us.

This is how every Christian and every local church can glorify God. But churches in need of revitalization almost inevitably have turned away from this commission to follow worldly pursuits. Every revitalization effort must culminate in the church being transformed to embrace the vision of growing as disciples and making other developing disciples. Unless this happens, the church will most certainly die.

The Two Journeys

The work of disciple-making is taught in the New Testament in the language of two journeys: the internal journey of growth into full maturity in Christ and the external journey of evangelism and missions.[1] The idea of the "two journeys" of evangelism and discipleship is taught throughout the New Testament, but it first became clear for me as I was preaching through the book of Philippians. In Philippians 1, Paul was writing to the Philippian church to encourage them that his imprisonment had "turned out for *the greater progress of the gospel*" (v. 12 NASB; emphasis mine) through his own evangelism of the praetorian guard and the increased boldness of watching Christians, who had lost their fear of punishment as a result of Paul's courageous example. He was also wrestling with his own future, whether he thought he would be executed or released. He became convinced that he would be released to continue his ministry of teaching and discipleship: "I will remain and continue with you all for your *progress and joy in the faith*" (Phil. 1:25; emphasis mine). Paul uses the same Greek word *progress* in Philippians 1:12 and 1:25, and the word implies a journey: (1) the progress *of* the gospel (evangelism and missions); and (2) progress *in* the gospel (discipleship toward full maturity in Christ).

These two journeys are absolutely intertwined. No healthy church can pick and choose between them, though sadly, most good churches tend to be imbalanced toward one or the other. Dying churches do neither. Perfect churches (of which there are none!) do each with perfect balance. Every revitalization effort must tend toward balanced progress in both of these journeys. If we turn away from either or both, we have taken steps toward the death of the church. Church leaders must understand these two journeys and effectively mobilize the members of the church to get up out of their pews and off their couches to begin running these twin journeys with faith and perseverance.

Missional Means Embracing Both Journeys

In Sebastian Junger's powerful book, *The Perfect Storm*, based on a true story, Billy Tyne captains the swordship *Andrea Gail*, manned by a team of fishermen who are desperate for a big catch. So Tyne decides to push out further east to the

Flemish Cap, a fertile fishing ground thirteen hundred miles from their home port of Gloucester, Massachusetts. There they land a stunning bonanza of swordfish, much to the joy of everyone on board. Their financial success seems guaranteed as they process the huge fish and begin packing them with ice for the voyage back home. But two problems doom the ship. First, the ice machine breaks, meaning the fish they have caught will go bad if they do not get back immediately. Second, a monster hurricane—the largest of the century—stands between them and their home. To save the fish from rotting, they decide to steam through the storm and end up being destroyed by waves in excess of one hundred feet.[2]

The failure of the ice machine is my point of connection here. Jesus sent us out to be "fishers of men" (Matt. 4:19), bringing lost souls to salvation in Christ. But if the fish "go bad" after being hauled into the boat, what is the point? Jesus did not send us merely to "land fish." He taught us to shepherd the flock all the way home. The essence of the external journey is setting people on their own internal journey. We are to make disciples and teach them to obey everything he has commanded—from justification, through sanctification, to glorification.

Many recent books on church revitalization do indeed embrace these two aspects of healthy church life somewhat. Nevertheless, I have noticed a tendency some of these writers and leaders have to place a strong emphasis on the external journey of evangelism and missions. They cannot seem to help saying things like, "The church exists to win the lost."[3] To be truly "missional" means to combine a missionary mind-set with the two journeys, not preferring either one or the other.

Ed Stetzer's *Comeback Churches* has a solid chapter on discipleship[4] that touches on most of the main areas of the internal journey. But even in that chapter, the goal always seems to be growth for the purpose of evangelism. Some churches go so far in their leaning toward the external journey that they neglect the internal journey and end up with massive problems among those who are "reached" with a shallow message of initial response to Christ. Bill Hybels, the leader of Willow Creek, acknowledged in an interview with *Christianity Today* in 2008 that this approach to ministry was woefully inadequate when it came to healthy discipleship of the many people who made professions of faith in Christ.[5]

I want to advocate a goal of pursuing a revitalized church with true balance between the internal journey of discipleship and the external journey of evangelism and missions.

Moving People on the Internal Journey of Discipleship

When a new pastor comes to a dying church, one of the first goals he should pray about and focus on is moving people toward a vibrant walk with Jesus Christ through the Holy Spirit. Many of the people in that church may well be unregenerate, despite years of faithfully attending church. The pastor should teach people the "marks of regeneration,"[6] ways by which people can know they're born again. He should also deliberately seek out conversations with each member to be certain that they are regenerate.

Beyond this, the revitalizing leader needs to have a clear vision of what a mature disciple is and how to move people toward that goal. I would recommend using my book *An Infinite Journey* as a road map toward spiritual maturity.[7] In it I argue that Christian maturity consists of Christlikeness in four major headings: knowledge, faith, character, and action (K-F-C-A).

- *Knowledge.* A mature disciple of Christ has a thorough, factual knowledge of the Bible and a rich heritage of experiential knowledge gained from daily life in the Spirit.
- *Faith.* A mature disciple of Christ has a strong and clear spiritual vision of unseen realities based on the Word of God—a strong sense that invisible things taught in the Bible are really true; a solid assurance of things hoped for based on the promises of God; a potent conviction over personal sin; an active reliance on Christ; and an accurate and biblically based sense of guidance from the Spirit.
- *Character.* A mature disciple of Christ has a heart conformed to Christ in what they love, hate, desire, choose, think, and feel.
- *Action.* A mature disciple of Christ lives a daily life of habitual obedience to God's Word, refusing to be polluted by sin, and actively obeying in main areas like worship, spiritual disciplines, family life, ministry to other Christians, missions to non-Christians, stewardship, and work.

I believe Scripture shows that biblical knowledge feeds faith, faith transforms character, and out of a transformed character, we walk in newness of life. This active lifestyle of obedience in turn feeds knowledge, resulting in a K-F-C-A cycle that drives individuals forward to make progress in the internal journey. All true revitalization efforts must be based on a similar comprehensive definition of discipleship toward mature Christlikeness.

These growing disciples will be the very ones who will use their spiritual gifts to build up the body of Christ, "When each part is working properly" (Eph. 4:16). They will be the very ones who will be sacrificially active in evangelizing their neighbors and bringing lost people to initial faith in Christ. Thus, the internal journey feeds the external journey. Jesus commanded that we "pray earnestly to the Lord of the harvest to send out laborers into his harvest" (Matt. 9:38). The ones who will obey and go are the ones who are following the internal journey path I just laid out.

Moving People on the External Journey of Mission

True church revitalization will inevitably result in the members rising up to embrace their responsibility to be witnesses to lost neighbors, co-workers, family members, and even total strangers. They will seek creative ways to serve the community's felt needs as a vehicle for displaying the love of God and for winning lost people to Christ.

Some key concepts all revitalizing leaders should communicate:

(1) *Root all evangelism in the glory of God.* Teach that God's glory is supreme (1 Cor. 10:31)—more important than even the value of a human soul—but show that the greatest display of God's glory in the universe is the salvation of sinners through faith in Christ.

(2) *Teach Christ's mission to save the lost.* Speak often of the verses in which Christ lays out his evangelistic mission: "The Son of Man came to seek and to save the lost" (Luke 19:10; see also Matt. 20:28; John 4:34; 6:39–40). Then connect them with our mission: "As the Father has sent me, even so I am sending you" (John 20:21). Let the Word of God do its convicting work!

(3) *Establish plainly the spiritual condition of the lost.* Demonstrate biblically that, apart from the saving grace of God in Christ, all people are lost, "Having no hope and without God in the world" (Eph. 2:12).

(4) *Show that the gospel of Christ is the only answer.* The exclusivity of Christ is central to the saving message of the Bible: "And there is salvation in no one else, for there is no other name under heaven given among men by which we must be saved" (Acts 4:12).

(5) *Connect the two great commandments to evangelism.* All God's law is summed up in "love God, and love your neighbor" (see Matt. 22:37–39). Regularly teaching the law will both reveal the sinfulness of all humanity (for no one keeps this law) and give us suitable motive for evangelism. We must be compelled by the love of Christ and love for our neighbor (2 Cor. 5:14–15).

(6) *Train people in the gospel message.* In a dying church, the people have almost certainly never been carefully trained in evangelism—either in the gospel message itself or in practical approaches to holding gospel conversations with people. Revitalizing leaders must do this careful work of training the people of the church to reach their mission fields.

(7) *Give people a vision for practical ministry that leads to evangelism.* The church must follow Jesus in meeting

present needs but always point to eternal, spiritual needs, for "What will it profit a man if he gains the whole world and forfeits his soul?" (Matt. 16:26). Missional churches find ways to connect with the surrounding community in which ministry to the body and soul are well-harmonized and properly proportioned. These ministries become a fruitful matrix of relationships in which the gospel can easily be shared.

(8) *Prepare the church for visitors.* As this training is going on, it is likely that more and more people will want to come to visit your church on a Sunday morning. Be ready to show them hospitality. Be ready to draw them into the life of the church.

(9) *Follow up with visitors.* If visitors willingly give contact information, it is their way of saying, "Please reach out to me." Such permission is like gold, so follow up with them.

(10) *Seek a "culture of evangelism" rather than programs.* Old patterns of program-based, "come and see" evangelism (tent revivals, events at the church, etc.) are not as effective as "go and tell" ministries in which people use their existing contacts with the lost to share the gospel.

(11) *Have people get specific about their own mission field.* To that end, the members of the church need to embrace their own mission field: workplace, neighborhood, children's activities (sports teams, music lessons, etc.). They need to be trained to think about lost people in their lives by name, and to begin praying for them and asking God how he wants them to reach out. They can use hospitality, inviting lost people to their homes. They can use mercy ministry, if the coworker or fellow student or neighbor has some medical emergency.

(12) *Cover all of this in prayer.* Regular and extraordinary prayer for evangelistic fruit should characterize the revitalization effort from the beginning and all the way through.

From a Dying Church to a Church Willing to Die for Christ

Making progress in the internal journey of spiritual growth in Christ is painful, constantly opposed by the world, the flesh, and the devil; even more painful is making progress in the external journey of evangelism and missions. There will be opposition, and there will be suffering. Dying churches have gotten to the sad state they are in because they selfishly loved their lives in this world and refused to take up their cross daily and follow Christ. They have become inwardly focused; they spend their money on themselves and their own comforts; they rarely invite people to church; they stopped looking for ways to engage the community and to serve its needs for the sake of the gospel. They have forgotten what Jesus taught: "Truly, truly, I say to you, unless a grain of wheat falls into the earth and dies, it remains alone; but if it dies, it bears much fruit" (John 12:24). As German pastor Dietrich Bonhoeffer put it, "When Jesus calls a man, he bids him, 'Come and die!'"[8]

We are part of a royal lineage of brothers and sisters who "loved not their lives even unto death" (Rev. 12:11). The early church spiritually conquered the Roman Empire in under three centuries because, as we said earlier, they were willing for their blood to be seed for the church. A revitalizing leader has to be effective in calling a dying church to start dying the right way: dying to selfishness, to sin, to earthly pleasures, to thinking that the church should serve them. The church has to die especially to caring what people will think if it shares the true gospel of Jesus Christ. As George Müller, the great evangelist, pastor, and coordinator of Christian orphanages in England put it: "There was a day when I died, utterly died—died to George Müller, his opinions, preferences, tastes, and will; died to the world, its approval or its censure; died to the approval or blame even of my brethren and friends—and since then I have only sought to show myself approved unto God."[9]

If the leaders can mobilize more and more members of the church to this level of self-denial, of dying daily for the cause of Christ, there will be more and more people from the community visiting the church, and more and more individuals brought to salvation in Christ. The church will no longer be dying shamefully but gloriously! For Jesus says, "Whoever loves his life loses it, and whoever hates his life in this world will keep it for eternal life" (John 12:25). The same is true of local churches.

Leading by Example

This burning zeal for the glory of God and for the plight of the lost must be clearly displayed in the evangelistic example of every revitalizing leader. You need to be regularly sharing the gospel with people in everyday life. You need to be personally strategizing how to meet and interact with more lost people, especially if you are in vocational ministry. You need to be able to say, "Be imitators of me, as I am of Christ" (1 Cor. 11:1).

Embracing Responsibility for the Unreached, Unengaged

Jesus made it clear that he will not return until the gospel is preached to the ends of the earth: "This gospel of the Kingdom will be preached in the whole world as a testimony to all nations, and then the end will come" (Matt. 24:14). Every healthy local church must embrace its responsibility in the external journey to the ends of the earth and to the end of time. William Carey was a missionary pioneer for the English Baptists. He organized a mission-sending agency to help him with his work reaching the lost in India. He said to his friends, "I will go down into the dark mine of heathenism, but you must hold the ropes."[10] We "hold the ropes" for missionaries by teaching every Christian's responsibility toward this global spread of the gospel. Even once dying churches can be revitalized to give sacrificially to the spread of the gospel to unreached, unengaged people groups (UUPGs) in other parts of the world. The essence of the disease that was leading toward the death of the church was a myopic selfishness that has forgotten God's purpose in the world. The leaders should speak often of missions, challenge the church to give, organize the church to pray for the UUPGs as various mission agencies report their needs.[11] For a church that was once nearing the grave to rise up covered with zeal for the lost to the ends of the world will greatly please and glorify our heavenly Father!

PRACTICAL ADVICE

1. Ask God to be glorified in the revitalization of your church in a healthy embracing of the making of disciples.

2. Understand the "two journeys" as explained in this chapter. Understand that all dead churches do not embrace either one of these journeys, and that even good churches tend to be imbalanced toward one or the other. Seek a healthy balance between faithful discipleship and courageous outreach.

3. Be gentle and patient with people who have never witnessed before. Follow the "key concepts" section of this chapter and teach these things patiently.

4. Ask the Lord to give you a specific vision for how your community can be reached. Start meeting people out in the public square. Frequent specific convenience stores, grocery stores, and malls to make acquaintances by name. Write those names down. Ask how you can pray for them. Be sure you do pray, and follow up the next week.

5. Invite people to church. Challenge church members to invite unchurched people to church.

6. Get church members into accountability relationships in which discipleship is the goal. Seek spiritual multiplication in the pattern of 2 Timothy 2:2. Use the K-F-C-A cycle to define and achieve spiritual maturity. Meet with key people for one year, and then tell them to meet with others in the same pattern you have used with them.

7. Have godly, mature women disciple younger women in the pattern of Titus 2. Pray for God to raise up such women or bring them to your church if there are none.

8. Preach and teach regularly Christ's heart for the lost, as I mentioned above.

9. Challenge each church member to have five names of people they are praying for. Tell them this is healthy accountability. Ask members who the five people are that they're lifting up in prayer. Be sure you also have five names.

10. Take people with you witnessing.

11. Ask the Lord to give church members practical ministries they can do that will engage them with lost people. Make sure these ministries have an evangelistic goal.

12. Trust the Lord for more and more people to baptize and disciple in the pattern of Matthew 28:18–20.

13. Give glory to God when he revitalizes the church with more and more new people!

17

A Heavenly Celebration of God's Glory

In the nineteenth century, British missionary C. T. Studd wrote these searching words: "Only one life, 'twill soon be past. Only what's done for Christ will last." I heard that brief poem long ago, and I have never forgotten it. Its message stands over me every single day and challenges me to "[redeem] the time, because the days are evil" (Eph. 5:16 KJV). I believe that the works we do for the glory of God on Earth will shine for all eternity in heaven.

As I was finishing the work for my bachelor's degree in mechanical engineering at MIT, I had to write a senior thesis of almost one hundred pages. At that time, I was still using a mechanical typewriter (I know I'm dating myself, but it's true!), and I had never heard of a word processor. Someone persuaded me to write the document at the computer lab, saying it would save me a ton of time. I went there, and the lab employees got me set up. I worked that day for hours and hours, writing a document that was due by the end of the week. I was under tremendous pressure, but I was productive and got twenty-four pages written—a very good day's work. Everything was great until a mysterious power surge came along and caused the computer to "blink." I had never used a computer to write a document before, and I had no idea about making a backup copy. Somehow, I had made one after the first page of writing, but that was all. I lost twenty-three pages of my work in one blink of an eye! I will never forget the pain of that moment. I was in utter despair. I tried to soldier up and start all over again at the top of page 2, but inky black depression came over me, and I went home for the day.

It was not until years later that the painful lesson became rooted for me as a powerful illustration of 1 Corinthians 3:12–15. Paul writes of the labor that various people had done in the local church at Corinth. Paul planted that church, others came after him to continue the "spiritual building project." Paul wrote to warn all who followed him that they needed to build skillfully and accurately, based wholly on their faithful ministry of the Word of God. He then asserted that, on Judgment Day, their works will all be tested:

> Now if anyone builds on the foundation with gold, silver, precious stones, wood, hay, straw—each one's work will become manifest, for the Day will disclose it, because it will be revealed by fire, and the fire will test what sort of work each one has done. If the work that anyone has built on the foundation survives, he will receive a reward. If anyone's work is burned up, he will suffer loss, though he himself will be saved, but only as through fire.

This passage teaches me that every church leader, indeed every Christian, will have their works tested by fire on Judgment Day. The works that are done well, faithful to Scripture, by the power of the Holy Spirit, for the glory of God, will survive the test and be displays of honor for both God and the worker for all eternity. The works that are done poorly—unbiblically, in a worldly manner, based on sin—will be consumed and will disappear forever. Like the twenty-three pages I lost in an instant that day at the MIT computer lab, so will be all my bad works. Gone . . . forever. The passage says I will suffer loss if any of my works are burned up. I yearn to avoid that loss. And I yearn, dear reader, for you to avoid that loss yourself.

If the Lord should choose to use us to revitalize a dying church for the praise of his glory, we will have the chance to celebrate his goodness and grace in that work for all eternity. Nothing that survives the fiery test of Judgment Day will ever disappear. We will be celebrating church history forever—not just our own works for God's glory but also what our brothers and sisters did. We will be so free from selfishness and pride in heaven that we will be able to celebrate God's works through us with perfect purity, as well as God's works through others with the same passion.

Some marvelous stories are still left to tell of revitalization all around the world! For all eternity, we will be studying one another's "crowns" even as we continually cast them down before Christ as ultimately belonging to him. May God empower you, dear reader, for the praise of his glory! May he speak the word *revitalize* to your church through your faithful ministry. I look forward to hearing your story when we get to heaven.

Notes

Chapter 1 Eyes of Blazing Fire: The Zeal of Christ to Revitalize His Church

1. The word *angel* means "messenger," and each of the letters Christ orders written to this or that church is written to the angel of that specific church. Christ would not be writing to a heavenly angel, so many interpreters feel that the angels of these seven churches are the elders or pastors of these churches. See John MacArthur, *New Testament Commentary: Revelation 1–11* (Chicago: Moody Press, 1999), 47–48.

2. "Five Trends among the Unchurched," Barna, October 9, 2014, http://www.barna.org/barna-update/culture/685-five-trends-among-the-unchurched.html.

3. Thom Rainer, "13 Issues for Churches in 2013," Church Leaders, accessed June 13, 2016, http://www.churchleaders.com/pastors/pastor-articles/164787-thom-rainer-13-issues-churches-2013.html.

4. Ed Stetzer and Mike Dodson, *Comeback Churches: How 300 Churches Turned Around and Yours Can Too* (Nashville: Broadman & Holman, 2007), xiii–xiv.

5. The largest church in America is Joel Osteen's Lakewood Church in Houston, TX, with significantly questionable theology in the "word of faith" pattern. See John MacArthur's critique of Joel Osteen quoted in Bill Combs, "Theologically Driven: Detroit Baptist Theological Seminary," September 22, 2014, http:www.dbts.edu/blog/john-macarthur-on-joel-osteen/.

Chapter 2 God Speaks Life into Dying Churches

1. Eighty percent of the Czech population has no religious affiliation at all, and surveys indicate about 1 percent are evangelical.

2. Sinclair B. Ferguson, David F. Wright, and J. I. Packer, ed., "Theology of Revival," in *New Dictionary of Theology* (Downer's Grove: Intervarsity Press, 1988).

215

3. Stephen Olford, *Heart-Cry for Revival: Expository Sermons on Revival* (Westwood, NJ: Revell, 1962), 33.

4. Earle Cairns, "Revival," in *Evangelical Dictionary of World Missions*, ed. A. Scott Moreau (Grand Rapids: Baker, 2000).

5. C. H. Spurgeon, "What Is a Revival," The Spurgeon Archive, accessed July 28, 2016, http://www.spurgeon.org/s_and_t/wir1866.php.

6. Mark Dever, *Nine Marks of a Healthy Church* (Wheaton, IL: Crossway, 2004).

7. J. I. Packer, *A Quest for Godliness: The Puritan Vision of the Christian Life* (Wheaton: Crossway Books, 1990), 298.

8. For more analysis of marks of a dying or dead church, see Thom Rainer, *Autopsy of a Deceased Church: 12 Ways to Keep Yours Alive* (Nashville: Broadman & Holman, 2014); also Harry L. Reeder III, *From Embers to a Flame: How God Can Revitalize Your Church* (Phillipsburg, NJ: P & R, 2008).

9. Tertullian said this is what the pagans would exclaim when they saw true Christians and how they interacted with one another. Quoted in Leon Morris, *The Gospel According to John* (Grand Rapids: Eerdmans, 1971), 485.

10. Rainer, *Autopsy*, 33.

Chapter 3 Embrace Christ's Ownership of the Church

1. Boniface (675?–754) was an Anglo-Saxon missionary to Germania. To counteract local pagan superstitions in Geismar, he assembled a crowd around the sacred oak of the Thundergod and began chopping down the tree. According to one legend, a powerful gust of wind came at that moment and blew the tree to the ground, confirming the power of Christ over the pagan gods. Ruth A. Tucker, *From Jerusalem to Irian Jaya: A Biographical History of Christian Missions* (Grand Rapids: Zondervan, 1983), 47–48.

2. Medical research has shown the beneficial effects of a fever on fighting viral or bacterial infections. The body can handle the elevated temperature far better than the pathogens. Paul Fassa, "Do Not Kill a Fever: Fever Kills Viruses," Natural News, October 2, 2009, http://www.naturalnews.com/027149_fever_virus_flu.html. In the same way, genuine Christians delight in more and more talk about the greatness of Jesus Christ and his kingship over all things. "Gospel hypocrites" (nominal Christians; unregenerate church members) cannot abide this elevated spiritual fervor.

Chapter 4 Be Holy

1. A. W. Tozer, *The Knowledge of the Holy* (San Francisco: HarperCollins, 1978), 70.

2. John Calvin, *The Institutes of the Christian Religion*, ed. John T. McNeill, trans. and indexed, Ford Lewis Battles, vol. 21 (Philadelphia: Westminster John Knox, 1960), 1.1.3.

3. Jonathan Edwards, "Personal Narrative," in *A Jonathan Edwards Reader*, eds. John E. Smith, Harry S. Stout, and Kenneth Minkema (New Haven: Yale University Press, 1995), 287–88.

4. Richard Baxter, *The Reformed Pastor* (Portland, OR: Multnomah, 1982), 28: "Take heed to yourselves, lest you live in those sins which you preach against in others, and lest you be guilty of that which daily you condemn. Will you make it your work to magnify God, and, when you have done, dishonor him as much as others? Will you proclaim Christ's governing power, and yet condemn it, and rebel yourselves? Will you preach his laws, and willfully break them? If sin be evil, why do you live in it if it be not, why do you dissuade men from it? If it be dangerous, how dare you venture on it? If it be not, why do you tell men so? If God's threatenings be true, why do you not fear them? If they be false, why do you needlessly trouble men, with them, and put them into such frights without a cause?"

Chapter 6 Rely on God's Word, Not on Techniques

1. Martin Luther, "Preface to the Complete Edition of Luther's Latin Writings; Wittenberg, 1545," in *Martin Luther: Selections from His Writings*, ed. John Dillenberger (New York: Anchor Books, 1961), 11.

2. Roland Bainton, *Here I Stand: A Life of Martin Luther* (New York: Abingdon Press, 1950), 185.

3. Timothy George, *The Theology of the Reformers* (Nashville: Broadman & Holman, 1988), 53.

4. Charles G. Finney, *Revival Lectures* (Grand Rapids, MI: Revell, 1993), 5.

5. Arnold Kurtz, "Charles G. Finney—Prototype of the Modern Evangelist," *Ministry*, November 1976, https://www.ministrymagazine.org/archive/1976/11/charles-g.-finney.

6. William G. McLoughlin Jr., *Modern Revivalism* (New York: The Ronald Press Company, 1959), 84.

7. Grace to You website slogan, http://www.gty.org/.

Chapter 7 Saturate the Church in Prayer

1. J. Edwin Orr, "Revival and Prayer," *Renewal Journal* 93, no. 1 (1993).

2. Matthew Henry on Zechariah 12:9–14 in *Matthew Henry's Commentary on the Whole Bible* (Peabody, MA: Hendrickson, 1991), 1590.

3. Jonathan Edwards, "On the Unreasonableness of Indetermination in Religion," Sermon on 1 Kings 18:21, in *Sermons and Discourses 1734–1738*, vol. 19 in *The Works of Jonathan Edwards*, ed. M. X. Lesser (New Haven: Yale University Press, 2001), 93.

4. David Martyn Lloyd-Jones, *Joy Unspeakable: Power and Renewal in the Holy Spirit* (Wheaton: Harold Shaw Publishers, 1984), 62.

5. I.D.E. Thomas, *A Puritan Golden Treasury* (Carlisle, PA: Banner of Truth Trust, 1977), 216.

6. Andrew Davis, *An Infinite Journey* (Greenville, SC: Ambassador, 2014), 225.

7. I heard Erwin Lutzer say this at a Gospel Coalition stakeholder's meeting. I looked it up online and found it attributed to many people, including Adrian Rogers. I'm not sure who first said it, but I first heard it from Lutzer.

8. Church Revitalization, *Forty Days of Prayer: Devotional Guide for Church Revitalization* (Grapevine, TX: Southern Baptists of Texas Convention, 2014), http://sbtexas.com/am-site/media/40-days-of-prayer.pdf.

9. John Piper, *Desiring God* (Portland, OR: Multnomah Books, 2003), 177.

Chapter 8 Cast a Clear Vision

1. Glenn Elert, ed., "Number of Colors Distinguishable by the Human Eye," published in 2006, http://hypertextbook.com/facts/2006/JenniferLeong.shtml; "101 Amazing Eye Facts," Lenstore Vision Hub, last accessed June 14, 2016, http://eyecare.lenstore.co.uk/101-amazing-eye-facts.

2. Davis, *Infinite Journey*, 45.

3. Dave Lavinsky, "Are You a Visionary Business Leader?" *Forbes*, April 26, 2013, http://www.forbes.com/sites/davelavinsky/2013/04/26/are-you-a-visionary-business-leader/.

4. *The Book on Leadership* (Nashville: Thomas Nelson, 2004), vii-viii: John MacArthur exposes numerous examples of Christian writers who cite secular business models of leadership and vision. He writes, "It is a serious mistake for Christians in positions of leadership to be more concerned with what is currently popular in the corporate world than what our Lord taught about leadership."

5. Andy Reinhardt, "Steve Jobs on Apple's Resurgence," *Business Week* (May 12, 1998): Steve Jobs said, "It's really hard to design products by focus groups. A lot of times, people don't know what they want until you show it to them."

6. John C. Maxwell, "The Four Practices of a Visionary Leader," accessed June 14, 2016, http://www.johnmaxwell.com/uploads/general/The_Four_Practices _of_a_Visionary_Leader.pdf.

7. Kenneth Copeland teaches the faith formula in these three easy steps: "All it takes is 1) seeing or visualizing whatever you need, whether physical or financial; 2) staking your claim on Scripture; and 3) speaking it into existence." http://thewordonthewordoffaithinfoblog.com/2013/03/17/the-secret-to-the-success-of -joel-osteen-and-the-prosperity-gospel/. Accessed September 11, 2015.

8. Ken Silva, "Joel Osteen and the Prosperity Gospel," October 25, 2012, Apprising Ministries, http://apprising.org/2012/10/25/joel-osteen-and-the-prosperity-gospel/.

Chapter 9 Be Humble toward Opponents

1. Keith Getty and Stuart Townend, "O Church Arise," ThankYou Music, 2005.

2. *Robert's Rules of Order* is a book written by Henry Martyn Robert and originally published in 1876 that is intended to be a handbook for directing meetings and making decisions as a group.

3. Bainton, *Here I Stand*, 185.

Chapter 10 Be Courageous

1. John Bunyan, *Pilgrim's Progress*, Section 2 in *The Works of John Bunyan*, vol. 3, ed. George Offor (Edinburgh: Banner of Truth Trust, 1991), 243.
2. The KJV of Mark 14:33 says Jesus was "sore amazed."
3. Davis, *Infinite Journey*, 233–34.
4. Tertullian, *Apologeticus*, in *Ante-Nicene Fathers*, vol. 3 (Peabody, MA: Hendrickson, 1995), 55.
5. Eusebius, "The Martyrdom of Polycarp," Church History IV. 15 in *Nicene and Post-Nicene Fathers*, vol. 1 (Peabody, MA: Hendrickson, 1995), 190.
6. Courtney Anderson, *To the Golden Shore: The Life of Adoniram Judson* (New York: Dolphin Books, 1956), 303–53.
7. A. G. Dickens, *The English Reformation*, 2nd ed. (University Park, PA: Pennsylvania State University Press, 1992), 99.

Chapter 11 Be Patient

1. My PhD advisor, the late Marvin Anderson, stated this several times in lectures at the Southern Baptist Theological Seminary. I have tried to track it down to an actual Luther quote in print, but I have been unable to do so. However, these words stuck with me in a powerful way through the events at FBC. The closest I could come to a Luther quote was in his writings against the iconoclastic riots of Wittenberg, February 1522, and against Andreas Bodenstein von Karlstadt.
2. Donald L. Miller, *The Story of World War II* (New York: Simon & Shuster, 2001), 188.
3. Charles Spurgeon, *Lectures to My Students* (Carlisle, PA: Banner of Truth, 2008), 394.
4. Ibid., 399.

Chapter 12 Be Discerning

1. Romans 14 speaks of "debatable issues" that Christians should not divide over: "As for the one who is weak in faith, welcome him, but not to quarrel over opinions" (Rom. 14:1). Romans 14 is a key chapter on how to maintain unity when discussing debatable issues that one should not break fellowship over.

Chapter 13 Wage War against Discouragement

1. This memorable expression refers to a morass of discouragement, and it comes from Bunyan, *Pilgrim's Progress*, 92.
2. Spurgeon, *Lectures*, 179.
3. Ibid.
4. Fred Meuser, "The Year Luther Quit Preaching," in *Logia: A Journal of Lutheran Theology*, vol. 3, no. 4 (October 1994): 67–68.
5. Spurgeon, *Lectures*, 179.
6. J. Herbert Kane, *The Legacy of J. Hudson Taylor*, April 1984, http://www .internationalbulletin.org/issues/1984-02/1984-02-074-kane.pdf.

7. Courtney Anderson, *To the Golden Shore: The Life of Adoniram Judson* (New York: Dolphin Books, 1961), 378.

8. John Piper, "Insanity and Spiritual Songs in the Soul of a Saint: Reflections on the Life of William Cowper," Desiring God, January 29, 1992, http://www.desiringgod.org/messages/insanity-and-spiritual-songs-in-the-soul-of-a-saint.

9. Jonathan Edwards, *The Life and Diary of the Rev. David Brainerd* in *The Works of Jonathan Edwards*, vol. 2 (Peabody, MA: Hendrickson Publishers, 2000), 354.

10. "What Missionaries Ought to Know about Depression," Missionary Care, accessed July 28, 2016, http://www.missionarycare.com/depression.html.

11. D. Martyn Lloyd-Jones, *Spiritual Depression: Its Causes and Cure* (Grand Rapids: Eerdmans, 1986), 20–21.

Chapter 14 Develop and Establish Men as Leaders

1. The most comprehensive defense for this doctrine of male leadership in the church in recent years has been John Piper and Wayne Grudem, eds., *Recovering Biblical Manhood and Womanhood: A Response to Evangelical Feminism* (Wheaton: Crossway Books, 1991). This excellent book thoroughly addresses the key biblical texts relevant to this issue, as well as arguments often made against it.

2. The term *elder* is interchangeable with "overseer" in Titus 1:6–7 and Acts 20:28.

Chapter 15 Become Supple on Worship

1. This was a famous expression used during the nineteenth century to speak of the worldwide expanse of the British Empire.

2. Willow Creek Community Church was founded in South Barrington, IL, in October 1975 by Bill Hybels. It has been a role model for the "seeker-sensitive" approach to church life in which the entire ministry is geared to making Christianity appealing to unchurched people.

3. Philip Ryken, Derek W. H. Thomas, Ligon Duncan, eds., *Give Praise to God: A Vision for Reforming Worship* (Phillipsburg, NJ: Presbyterian and Reformed, 2003), 475.

4. Leland Ryken, *Worldly Saints: The Puritans As They Really Were* (Grand Rapids: Zondervan, 1990), 122.

Chapter 16 Embrace the Two Journeys of Disciple-Making

1. *Evangelism* is the proclamation of the gospel of Jesus Christ to someone within our own culture and language. *Missions* is the proclamation of the same gospel to people from other cultures and languages.

2. Sebastian Junger, *The Perfect Storm* (New York: W. W. Norton, 2000), 177.

3. Tim Keller, *The Missional Church*, June 2001, http://download.redeemer.com/pdf/learn/resources/Missional_Church-Keller.pdf: "Some churches certainly carried out evangelism as one ministry among many, but the church in the West had not become completely *missional*—adapting and reformulating absolutely

everything it did in worship, discipleship, community, and service so as to be engaged with the non-Christian society around it"; quoted by Ed Stetzer, *Comeback Churches*, 7.

4. Ed Stetzer, "Connecting People to Spiritual Maturity," in *Comeback Churches*, 117–30.

5. Matt Branaugh, "Willow Creek's 'Huge Shift': Influential Megachurch Moves Away from Seeker-Sensitive Services," *Christianity Today*, May 15, 2008, http://www.christianitytoday.com/ct/2008/june/5.13.html.

6. Second Corinthians 13:5 says, "Examine yourselves, to see whether you are in the faith. Test yourselves. Or do you not realize this about yourselves, that Christ Jesus is in you?—unless indeed you fail to meet the test!" No movement of people in church history was as careful and practical as the Puritans in relation to helping people obey this text. They made careful lists of "marks of regeneration" by which people could see if God's grace had worked savingly in their souls. They usually began with lists of false marks, signs which are no proof either way of genuine conversion. Then they would proceed to various marks that centered around willingness to examine yourself, personal holiness (especially in secret), love for God's Word, love for Christ, love for God's people, freedom from habitual sin, perseverance through trials, etc. Joel Beeke and Mark Jones have given a brief overview of these Puritan themes in "The Puritans on Regeneration," in *Puritan Theology: Doctrine for Life* (Grand Rapids: Reformed Heritage Books, 2012), 463–80.

7. Davis, *Infinite Journey*, 31.

8. Dietrich Bonhoeffer, *The Cost of Discipleship* (New York: Scribner, 1963), 7.

9. A. T. Pierson, *George Müller of Bristol: His Life of Prayer and Faith* (Grand Rapids: Kregel, 1999), 367.

10. Julia H. Johnstone, *Fifty Missionary Heroes Every Boy and Girl Should Know* (New York: Revell, 1913), 11.

11. JoshuaProject.net; the Southern Baptist Convention's International Mission Board's website, www.imb.org/pray.

Andrew Davis is senior pastor of First Baptist Church in Durham, North Carolina. He holds degrees from the Massachusetts Institute of Technology (BSME, 1984), Gordon-Conwell Theological Seminary (MDiv, 1990), and the Southern Baptist Theological Seminary (PhD in Church History, 1998). He worked for ten years as a mechanical engineer, and he was a church planter in Massachusetts and Japan before coming to this pastorate in 1998. He and his wife, Christi, have five children.

THE GOSPEL **COALITION**

*Advocate for Gospel-Centered
Principles and Practices*

To learn more, visit:
www.TheGospelCoalition.org